SMALLVILLE

SEASON 2

THE OFFICIAL COMPANION

Superman created by Jerry Siegel and Joe Shuster

SMALLVILLE: THE OFFICIAL COMPANION SEASON 2
1 84023 947 6

Published by
Titan Books
A division of
Titan Publishing Group Ltd
144 Southwark St
London
SE1 0UP

First edition March 2005
10 9 8 7 6 5 4 3 2 1

Visit our websites:
www.titanbooks.com
www.dccomics.com

Did you enjoy this book? We love to hear from our readers.
Please e-mail us at: readerfeedback@titanemail.com
or write to Reader Feedback at the above address.

To subscribe to our regular newsletter for up-to-the-minute news, great offers and competitions, email: titan-news@titanemail.com

A CIP catalogue record for this title is available from the British Library.

Printed and bound in Great Britain by MPG, Cornwall.

SMALLVILLE

SEASON 2

THE OFFICIAL COMPANION

Paul Simpson

TITAN BOOKS

Thanks are once again due to many people for their help in preparing this book. It wouldn't be possible without the cooperation of all those members of the cast and crew who so graciously gave up their limited free time to be interviewed on and off set; Kendra Crowther in Vancouver, Lisa Rose and Susan Kesser in L.A. for coordination above and beyond the call of duty; the Anglo-American Alliance (Katrina Gerhard, Jerry Boyaijan, Jenn Fletcher and Cherry Greveson) for the visual material; the Sophie Brigade (Clare & Vince, Joe & Kate, Felicity, Anali, Lucinda and Katherine) for keeping an eye out when my concentration was elsewhere; Helen Grimmett and Sharon Gosling for helping turn hours of interviews into practical material; Tracy Morgan and Andy Lane for their support during all the upheaval; Mark Warshaw for research material; Craig Byrne for all his help on and off the Web; Rich Matthews for morale-boosting; Jo Boylett for her editing skills; Marcus Scudamore and Evie Joannou for their design expertise; and to Adam Newell at Titan and Chris Cerasi at DC Comics who continue to keep the faith.

Special thanks as ever to Alfred Gough and Miles Millar for being available to discuss it despite the many other calls on their time, and to Joe Shuster and Jerry Siegel for such a fantastic template. — Paul Simpson

The publishers would like to thank the following people who contributed to the *Torch* and *Ledger* articles featured in this book: Jake Black, Angela Dai'Re, Christopher Freyer, Lisa Gregorian, Karen Miller, Gena Murph, Will Rogers, Mimi Soo and Kathryn Zoucha. The publishers would also like to thank Phyllis Hume and Steve Korté at DC Comics, and the entire production team of *Smallville* for all their help with this project.

Publisher's note: The interviews in this book were conducted before the sad passing of Christopher Reeve in October 2004.

DEDICATION
This one's for Kara-Leigh, a friendly face in a faraway place.

CONTENTS

FOREWORD

Clark and Lana have been sucked into a twister. Lex is poised to watch his father die. Jonathan is lost in the eye of the storm. Clark's spaceship has hummed to life. What the hell were we thinking? To be honest, we had no idea how we were going to wrap everything up. Somehow we did, and opened season two in high gear and even higher ratings.

The second season introduced red kryptonite and, with it, a side of Clark that we hadn't seen before. Um… a leather jacket? And you thought Clark was strictly a flannel man. The scene in the Sex Ed class was something we had written for the pilot, but had cut at the last second because of the ballooning budget. Lucky for us, it turned out to be the inspiration for one of the best episodes of the series.

We also thought it was time for someone outside the Kent household to learn Clark's secret. Of course, being Superman's best friend isn't always easy. Having Pete find the spaceship and discover Clark's alien origin was a huge decision. But we felt it gave us a whole new dimension to explore with these characters. We were eager to examine the power of friendship and loyalty… and the price of having to keep a secret. As many super heroes know, with power comes great responsibility, and as Lionel Luthor would tell you, there are few greater powers than knowledge.

Season two also saw the introduction of Dr. Virgil Swann. We had always dreamed that Christopher Reeve would one day be on the show, and felt this was the right time to do it. So we called his agent and were delighted when Chris agreed to guest star. We really wanted to create a role that was worthy of Chris and the legacy of his work as Superman. Hence, Dr. Virgil Swann was born. It felt natural that Chris should be the one who opened

Below: Pete learns Clark's secret in season two.

Clark's eyes to his past and future. Dr. Swann provided the first tantalizing answers to the questions that had been plaguing Clark for all of his young life. Where am I from? What happened to my parents? Am I truly alone?

The production challenges of actually filming the scenes with Chris were enormous. Chris had an unbelievably busy schedule, and it was too expensive to have him fly up to Vancouver with his medical team. So we decided to bring Smallville to him. We flew Tom and director/producer Greg Beeman out to New York. John Wells kindly agreed to let us use the basement prop room of his NBC show *Third Watch* as our set. Chris was a total pro and worked non-stop for twelve hours, and even had time for a press conference and PSA. It was truly an inspiring experience, and one that everybody involved with the show will always be proud of. We are honored to have known him.

Above: Tom Welling and Christopher Reeve during the filming of 'Rosetta' in New York.

The second season brought with it a lot of changes, both on and off the screen. We gained some new writers who have since become stalwarts of the show, Todd Slavkin & Darren Swimmer, Brian Peterson & Kelly Souders, as well as comic book god Jeph Loeb (because he knew a little something about Superman). Ken Biller also joined the show and proved to be a dynamic force in the writers' room and behind the camera, quickly becoming one of our best directors. A special thank you to Lisa Lewis: we couldn't have pulled off the New York shoot without her incredible tenacity and dedication. Thanks to all the unsung heroes who work behind the scenes of the show both in Vancouver and in Los Angeles. You always rise to the challenges we set you. It is no exaggeration to say that *Smallville* really does have one of the best crews in the business. Thanks, guys.

Finally, we want to thank you, the fans. Thanks for watching. Thanks for telling us when we do good and when we mess up. Always know that we are striving to make the show as great as it can be. ▪

Alfred Gough & Miles Millar
Los Angeles, January 2005

INTO SEASON TWO

CLARK SUPERSPEEDS
down the road, searching for Lana's truck. The wind batters him from every angle, dirt
blasts his face like buckshot. He forces himself onward, heads over a hill to see

THE MASSIVE TWISTER
converging on

THE PICKUP TRUCK
which is rocking back and forth, about to be sucked into the vortex. Lana is in the
front, gripping the wheel in absolute terror. She locks eyes with Clark.

                              LANA
                Claaaaaaaaaaaaaaaaaaaaaaaaaaark!

But at that moment the truck is suddenly

LIFTED OFF THE GROUND
and sent spiraling into the funnel. Clark unleashes an AGONIZING WAIL.

                              CLARK
                Laaaaaaaaaaaaaaaannnaaaaaaaaaa!

As the truck disappears into the churning tornado and Clark blurs into the eye of the
storm, the words...

                        "TO BE CONTINUED"

...flash on-screen and, we...

SMASH CUT TO: END OF FIRST SEASON

"What was interesting about coming into season two was that we already had a fair amount of ideas that we'd held off from using during season one," executive producer Al Gough explains. "We were able to get good momentum going into the season because of that. After episode nine of season one, we had found our sea legs, and we just kept moving. Season two became a continuation of that."

Inevitably there were some changes in personnel between the seasons. On-screen these were marked by the recut title sequence which removed scenes featuring Eric Johnson as Whitney Fordman, whose character would return for one final bow during the year, and incorporated John Glover's Lionel Luthor, reflecting the increasingly important part that the businessman would play during the second season.

Behind the scenes, Gough and his writing and producing partner, Miles Millar, brought in writer and director Ken Biller to run the writers' room. "During season

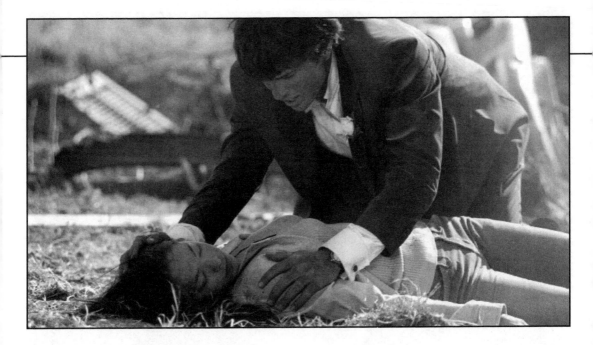

Above: Clark tends to the unconscious Lana.

one, Miles and I wrote the final draft of every episode," Gough notes. "That's what happens during the first season of a show when you're finding your show and its voice. But we've always believed that television is a team sport, and I think in order to function as human beings you need writing staff. I also think you need writing staffs to expand your show. You need to hire staff that you can then rely on and take and bring the show to the next level. As a writer you only have so many tricks in your bag. It's always about expanding the world and deepening the relationships."

Legendary comic book scribe Jeph Loeb was one of the writers who joined the show at the start of the new year. "We spent the first two weeks just coming up with ideas," he remembers. "'What if we did this? What if we did that? This story's never been told... What characters in *Smallville* have we not explored — teacher, milkman, mailman, farmer...? We filled up white board after white board of all those ideas before we started pitching actual stories."

The special effects changed as well for the second year, with Entity FX taking over responsibility for that vital part of the show. The Santa Monica-based company had just finished working on *The X-Files* when "we got a call asking if we would be interested in working on *Smallville*," visual effects supervisor Mat Beck recalls. "We do all kind of projects: films, commercials and videos, and we like doing episodic television."

Although season two comprised twenty-three episodes, principal photography for 'Redux' had been completed at the end of the first season, immediately after shooting finished on 'Tempest' and before the cast and crew took a well-deserved break. But they were soon back at the studios in the east Vancouver suburb of Burnaby, with director Greg Beeman ready to shoot Clark Kent's first adventure away from the confines of gravity... ■

THE EPISODES

"You won't find the answers by looking to the stars. It's a journey you'll have to take by looking inside yourself. You must write your own destiny... Kal-El."

— Dr. Virgil Swann to Clark

SEASON 2 REGULAR CAST:

Tom Welling (Clark Kent)

Kristin Kreuk (Lana Lang)

Michael Rosenbaum (Lex Luthor)

John Schneider (Jonathan Kent)

Annette O'Toole (Martha Kent)

Allison Mack (Chloe Sullivan)

Sam Jones III (Pete Ross)

John Glover (Lionel Luthor)

VORTEX

WRITTEN BY: Philip Levens STORY BY: Alfred Gough & Miles Millar DIRECTED BY: Greg Beeman	GUEST STARS: Tom O'Brien (Roger Nixon), Mitchell Kosterman (Sheriff Ethan)

Somehow able to propel himself through the tornado, Clark rescues Lana from the pickup truck and superspeeds her to the hospital. Lex pulls his father free from the rubble, but Lionel is seriously injured, and Lex agrees to emergency surgery to save his sight. The operation, however, is a failure.

Caught in the storm, Jonathan and Nixon get trapped in a crypt underneath a motor home. The reporter lets Jonathan destroy the videotape in exchange for a way out. Lex helps Clark search for his father and tries to get in touch with Nixon. When Jonathan hears Lex's voice, he destroys Nixon's cell phone, while above ground Clark becomes suspicious of Lex. However, the call limits the search area, since only one transmission mast still stands. As they search, Clark and Chloe decide to just be friends, much to Chloe's sorrow.

Old maps of the area show the crypt's location, and Clark rushes there. But the crypt is full of meteor rocks, and Nixon tries to use them to keep Clark subdued so he can present the young man as evidence. Jonathan and Nixon fight once more, and just as the reporter gets the upper hand, Lex shoots him. Still suspicious, Jonathan nevertheless agrees to a fresh start with Lex.

CLARK: That's the second time you hesitated today, Lex. I'm starting to wonder if what my dad said about you is true.

"The first five minutes of 'Vortex' solved the cliffhanger from season one," executive producer Al Gough explains, "and then we spent the rest of that episode setting up what the dynamics were going to be for season two: Lana's distrust of Clark; what happened to the spaceship, which became Clark looking into his origins; Lex protecting Clark and killing the reporter; and the Lex/Lionel dynamic, with Lionel being blind."

Physical effects supervisor Mike Walls considers 'Vortex' "probably the best work I've ever done. I don't think any other show can come close to the opening sequence of the episode. Greg Beeman was phenomenal throughout — he knew exactly what he wanted from the get-go, and he explained it perfectly."

Beeman himself agrees that "the first five minutes are spectacular. We were very proud of the way we introduced certain tools to the filmmaking process. We agitated the film and all the camerawork was handheld. The fight with Jonathan and Roger Nixon in the storm and Clark in the tornado were great, and all very difficult to execute."

Opposite: Clark surveys the tornado damage.

Smallville 🐓 Ledger

★ ★ ★ Volume 64, Number 14 ★ ★ ★

LIONEL LUTHOR AMONG THE INJURED
Couldn't Have Happened to a Nicer Guy, Town Says

Kansas residents have long known that tornadoes don't adhere to class distinctions: they're equal-opportunity destroyers. Smallville's citizens need only look up at the wind-blasted Luthor mansion to confirm that credo.

Lex Luthor's ancestral home stood for centuries in Scotland and survived a transatlantic crossing, only to find itself situated on one of the most dangerous plots in America. Now, gaping holes mark the former location of broad, intricate stained-glass windows, and piles of rubble are all that's left of some of the ornate turrets and overhangs.

But just as the storm claimed shacks and castles alike, it attacked farmhands and billionaires with the same rage. Reports soon reached the media that LuthorCorp capo Lionel Luthor was in town when the twisters converged, and he was among the wounded lining the overcrowded halls of Smallville Medical Center — alongside, ironically, some of the thousands of people he and his son had recently thrown into unemployment with the devastating closure of LuthorCorp Fertilizer Plant No. 3.

By Jim 'Slim' Bradlee

Visual effects producer Mat Beck, of Santa Monica-based Entity FX, took over responsibility for the visual effects in the second season. "You're fighting the battle to make *Smallville* as exciting and otherworldly and perilous as it can be, pushing the bounds of reality," he explains. His first episode in charge was certainly a baptism of fire. "In 'Vortex', we were pushing the camera into a truck that's spinning around in the center of a tornado, and the truck is being assaulted so that pieces are falling off!" he remembers. The tornado was created from various elements. "We used animated sprites of real smoke that flew around following particles," Beck says. "It was the perfect thing — it combined God's rendering system with ours. It had an organic look, while we could make it do what we wanted it to do. The interior of the tornado was created by Tony Smoller, who did a marvelous bit of quick work to create the dimensionality and chaos inside there. We used a lot of shaking camera. John Wash, our visual effects guy on the set, shot a bunch of debris hanging in front of a green screen, so we had straw and mailboxes which we could swirl around. Jon Han built the truck on the computer. But not just a truck — he built an engine block and fenders, which all had to rip off. We shot the real Clark and Lana on a partial truck with tracking marks on it, and then tracked a computer generated truck around them, so we could drag it off piece by piece." The stunning results onscreen were well worth the effort.

'Time and Time Again'
by Stretch Princess
'In My Place' by Coldplay

Above: Clark and Lex try to define the search area.

"I love the moment when Lex kills Nixon," says Greg Beeman. "Nixon reacts, blood comes out of his chest, he falls, and that reveals Lex. Then the camera pushes in on Michael. He said that it was really important that there was a close-up of him. I didn't give him any specific direction, but you can legitimately interpret what he did in two ways: either Lex is horrified and appalled, or he liked it, and it felt good to him. That's what I love about Rosenbaum, how subtle and nuanced his performance is." Al Gough points out that "we purposely didn't have Lex shoot anybody in the first season. At one point in 'Rogue', he was going to shoot Phelan, but we didn't want to get to that point yet."

NIXON: Do you have any idea what I would do with his abilities? The wealth, the power he could amass. It's unimaginable.
JONATHAN: You are exactly the reason why I keep his abilities a secret.

"Did he like it? Didn't he like it? No one really knows," Michael Rosenbaum says. "That's how I wanted you to feel. There are a lot of ways you can look at it, and all of them work. If he killed when he was younger, for whatever reason, this could be the first time since. And he remembers pulling the trigger before. It has scared and upset him that he's had to do this again. Or was this his first time? And it felt good — didn't it?"

"'Vortex' is the most amazing hour of television I've seen," John Schneider concludes. "It moves like crazy!" ∎

DID YOU KNOW?

The title sequence was changed for this episode, with new clips added, as well as marking Eric Johnson's departure and John Glover's arrival as a recurring character.

HEAT

WRITTEN BY: Mark Verheiden
DIRECTED BY: James Marshall

GUEST STARS: Krista Allen (Desiree Atkins-Luthor),
Mitchell Kosterman (Sheriff Ethan)

DID YOU KNOW?

Guest star Krista Allen played prostitute Kristy Hopkins in three early episodes of *CSI: Crime Scene Investigation*, and has also appeared in *Charmed* and *Baywatch Hawaii*.

The start of the new school year is marked by the arrival at Smallville High of a hot new teacher, Desiree Atkins, who Clark is amazed to hear is Lex's fiancée. Her sex education lesson is interrupted when Clark develops a new power, heat vision, which he finds impossible to control. After nearly being responsible for burning down the Talon with Lana inside, Clark asks his father for help, and eventually he gets the power in check. Desiree is able to control Lex using meteor-enhanced pheromones, and she persuades him to tear up the pre-nuptial agreement before they get married. After she fails to seduce Clark, she frames him for arson. She then turns her attention to Jonathan Kent, who she persuades to kill Lex, but Clark escapes from jail in time to use his heat vision to melt the bullet from Jonathan's rifle.

Meanwhile, Lana, who is sending a video message to Whitney, realizes it's time for her to be honest with him about her feelings.

MARTHA: How was school?

CLARK: It was different.

JONATHAN: Do we like different?

"*Smallville* is always about puberty with superpowers," Al Gough explains. "I like any time that we can play the superpowers as a metaphor for teen problems, whether it's acne or premature ejaculation!"

The executive producers had always intended to give Clark heat vision. "Actually, at one point we introduced it in the pilot," Gough recalls. "It was in a very early draft of the script, again with the idea of it arriving in the sex ed class, but then we thought, 'Why are we spoiling this? Let's save it.' It also took us a season until we saw, in terms of visual effects, a heat vision that we liked. We didn't want to do the red beams out of the eyes. X-ray vision had always been 'see-through' vision with Superman, and we wanted X-*ray* vision; in the same way, we wanted heat vision with this."

"It wasn't laser vision," Miles Millar amplifies. "We wanted to have a power that Clark could use in front of other people. They wouldn't necessarily be aware he was using it — it was almost invisible. We liked the idea of distorting the frame and having a heat ripple."

"Al and Miles are very smart in terms of what they wanted," visual effects supervisor John Wash comments. "They wanted it to be fairly accurate in terms of what you might see from something that was searingly hot traveling through the air, like a disturbance of the atmosphere. We keyed our research off the little ripples that you see if a light goes past a hotplate and reflects on a wall. We used the computer to create a conical version

Opposite: Clark ponders his fate.

DID YOU KNOW?

Some of Chloe's adventures while working at the *Daily Planet* during the summer between 'Vortex' and 'Tempest' were chronicled in the *Smallville* comic book.

of that effect that could emanate from Clark's eyes, in combination with a little iris effect."

"There are great parallels between life and art with heat vision," Mat Beck adds. "We were trying to find a cool way to do heat vision at the same time as Clark was trying to figure out how to control it. It went through a bunch of versions while we got it the way Miles and Al wanted it. Al wanted the things to be almost blobs of heat vision rather than always a consistent ray. He wanted the snaky feeling that it was out of control. We had these blobs of heat hit the screen when he was watching the film, literally igniting the screen."

Co-executive producer Ken Biller, who headed the writers' room for the second season, regards 'Heat' as "one of my favorite episodes. Mark Verheiden wrote a terrific

Opposite: Clark uses his heat vision to save the day for the first time.

Smallville ⬛ Ledger

* * * Volume 64, Number 15 * * *

TEEN ARSON SUSPECT 'RELEASED'

A local high school student was released from jail after being detained on suspicion of setting fire to a car in the Smallville High School parking lot.

Clark Kent was arrested for arson after Desiree Atkins, a teacher at SHS and the wife of local tycoon Lex Luthor, reported seeing Kent set her car on fire last night. According to Atkins, Kent doused her car with gasoline and tossed a lit match at the vehicle. The car exploded in flames and then flipped over.

Atkins, who said she was at the school working late, allegedly witnessed the incident as she was walking toward the parking lot. "He didn't know I was there, but I was too scared and stunned to try to stop him," said Atkins. "I just stood there and watched him blow up my car." Atkins was not injured in the incident. Although the fire occurred after hours, Atkins claimed she had several students ready to confirm her story.

By Eric Miller

script that was a fun balance between humor and serious subject matter. It was a quintessential way to take the metaphor of adolescence that the show had established so brilliantly in the pilot, and extrapolate it."

CLARK: What would you say if I told you Miss Atkins, aka Alison Sanders, showed up at my loft last night and tried to seduce me.

CHLOE: I'd say you were living the voyeuristic fantasy of every male student in this school.

"It was a lot of fun to write," Verheiden confirms. "We wanted to have a good time with it, coming out of 'Vortex' and 'Tempest' which had been pretty heavy. We wanted to re-establish that the kids are back at school, and re-establish that they're teenagers." The episode is very clearly set three months after the events of 'Vortex'. "If you're doing a show for a teen network, it helps to play the real time of the school year," Al Gough notes. "And we didn't want to then play the summer, because quite honestly, we didn't have the weather up in Vancouver!"

"The challenge of that episode was 'selling' the heat," recalls production designer David Willson, who also joined the show at the start of the second year. "Fortunately we had quite a hot spell at the time, but we had a lot of fans in the scenes. Plus everybody was in flimsy summer gear." ▪

SMALLVILLE MUSIC

'Tomorrow' by Avril Lavigne
'Truth or Dare' by N.E.R.D.
'A Little Less Conversation' by Elvis
'Hot In Herre' by Nelly
'My Friend's Over You' by New Found Glory

DUPLICITY

WRITTEN BY: Todd Slavin
& Darren Swimmer
DIRECTED BY: Steve Miner

GUEST STARS: Joe Morton (Dr. Steven Hamilton),
Sarah-Jane Redmond (Nell Potter), Andrew Jackson
(Ray Wallace), Michael Kopsa (Dean), Cameron Cronin
(Dr. Glenn)

DID YOU KNOW?

Though Pete Ross's modern comics incarnation doesn't know that Clark Kent is Superman — even though he's married to Lana Lang, who does! — in the pre-1986 Superman continuity, the young Pete did know that Clark Kent was Superboy.

After being fired by Lex, renegade scientist Dr. Hamilton — who has now become affected by meteor-induced jitters — runs truck driver Ray Wallace off the road. When Pete stops to help Wallace, he finds Clark's spaceship in the field. He gets Clark to help him hide it at his house. Meanwhile, Dr. Hamilton has learned of the spaceship's discovery and kills the driver to get Pete's name, then steals the ship. The Kents go to retrieve the ship, but it's gone, and they are spotted by Pete. When Pete confronts him, Clark realizes he has no option, and tells his friend the truth. Pete is furious and storms off. Hamilton tries to get the key back from Lex, but Lex claims it was lost in the tornado. The scientist then persuades the blinded Lionel Luthor, who has come to Smallville to escape from the doctors, to come 'see' the ship. Lionel tells Hamilton that if he can open the ship, his research will be funded. Hamilton kidnaps Pete to try to get the key, but the teenager refuses to tell him anything. Clark comes to Pete's rescue, and Hamilton literally jitters himself to death.

Meanwhile, Lana's aunt Nell tells Lana that her boyfriend Dean has asked her to marry him.

PETE: Sure, Chloe. I saw a spaceship. I even met an alien.
CHLOE: Really? Would you like to describe it?
PETE: Actually, he looks a lot like Clark.

"Pete just seemed like the odd man out," Al Gough comments. "So him learning the secret was something that we decided we needed to do in order to give that character a function on the show. We thought that was a good way to plug him in a little more and give Clark somebody other than his parents to talk to."

"That was a directive from Al and Miles going into the season," Ken Biller recalls. "It's a really strong emotional story about that friendship, and a turning point for Clark."

"Pete's reaction to Clark is really good," Gough adds. "We said, 'Honestly, if Clark said this to Pete, what would Pete's first reaction be?' and it wasn't, 'Oh great, let's be friends.' We really wanted to play the emotions of that discovery and revelation on Pete. Sam and Tom both did a really terrific job."

"'Duplicity' was a big visual effects episode," production designer David Willson recalls. "Whenever we have big, expensive visual effects, we're always challenged on the production design end to try to make things work on the soundstage. We don't have the money to go on location, or do a big new set for Hamilton's lab. We redressed the barn for that."

Opposite: Clark looks down in worry at Pete's discovery.

'Southbound Train' by Travis Tritt

'Ordinary' by Greg Jones

'Leading With My Heart'
   by Alice Peacock

'Goodbye' by Stephanie Simon

SMALLVILLE TORCH

Volume 52, Number 3

SMALLVILLE STUDENT RESCUES MOTORIST

It began as just an average day for Smallville High student Pete Ross. He did not expect to become a hero by nightfall. But that is exactly what occurred last week when Ross pulled Ray Wallace, owner of Ray's Lock and Key, from Wallace's crashed pickup truck in a cornfield off Loeb Bridge Road. Ross rushed a seriously injured Wallace to Smallville Medical Center.

I spoke with the young hero shortly after the incident. Ross said, "I'm glad I was able to help him. It seems like a lot of accidents occur here in town. People get distracted too easily while they drive. It's a good thing I was there for Ray. I hate to think of what could have happened…"

Ray Wallace survived his injuries but overdosed on morphine while recuperating at the medical center. He passed away two nights ago. His employees and family have expressed their gratitude to Pete for his heroic efforts on Ray's behalf.

By Jake Black

Mat Beck notes that the episode was challenging, because the effects team had to help explain what happened to the rest of the meteor rock serum after Clark tackled Dr. Hamilton. "The glowing green stuff didn't photograph well, so we had to help it in post-production," he explains. "We used computer graphics to stick the syringe into the rope that tied Pete up, and then broke the end off, so we could get the syringe out without it creating a bunch of drops all over his clothing, which we'd then have to track."

JONATHAN: Pete… I'm proud of you. But I do hope you realize what a tremendous responsibility knowing this secret is. And believe me, it's not going to get any easier.

CLARK: That's my dad's way of saying welcome to the family.

The sequence also saw Clark's intense reaction to the meteor rocks. Although it might seem as if the most sensible way to do that would be for the visual effects people to add the rippling veins in post-production, in fact it's done in reverse. "Those shots are difficult — as simple a moment as it is," Mat Beck explains. "People have a high expectation of reality for anything to do with human skin, because we spend our lifetime looking at it. We've worked out a technique where John Wash puts some prosthetic veins on Tom's hands on the set, which of course move when he moves, and we augment them by adding the glow. But we also 'hide' the veins digitally for the shots where he's not affected. Sometimes in visual effects, the solution involves thinking upside down, backwards or sideways."

There are other times when the visual effects team expects to have to do something,

Opposite: Clark reveals his powers to Pete.

and discover that they aren't required after all. "We were prepared to do a gag on Joe Morton, to make him look like he was shaking," Beck recalls, "but the combination of the under-cranked camera [shooting fewer frames per second than usual, which speeds up the action when it's played back at normal speed] and his natural shaking looked great."

Greg Beeman still wonders whether Lionel Luthor really was quite as he seemed in this episode. "In retrospect, we don't know whether he ever really was blind, or whether he was blind briefly and it healed," he notes. "What did Lionel see? What does he know? It's one of the big questions in *Smallville*'s history." ∎

DID YOU KNOW?

Listen for Pete humming the theme from *The X-Files* — written by *Smallville*'s composer Mark Snow.

RED

WRITTEN BY: Jeph Loeb
DIRECTED BY: Jeff Woolnough

GUEST STARS: Sara Downing (Jessie Brooks), Michael Tomlinson (U.S. Marshal), Garwin Sanford (Mr. Brooks), Daryl Shuttleworth (Deputy Principal)

DID YOU KNOW?

The Loeb Bridge, where Lex hits Clark in his Porsche, was named after Jeph Loeb. Before his job title of consulting producer was agreed, Jeph joked that he should be credited on the show as 'Ambassador to Spain'.

When Clark puts on his new red class ring, his personality changes instantly. He flirts with a new pupil, Jessie, gets bored with studying, and asks Pete if he wants to go to a bar. He even goes to Metropolis and spends a fortune on the Kents' credit cards. When Jonathan confronts him, he pushes him away. Chloe discovers that the rings are made from a red version of the meteor rock, and the Kents realize that this has affected Clark emotionally. Clark borrows Lex's car to take Lana to a bar, but she is disgusted by his behavior, and leaves him there. He turns his attentions to Jessie, who is also there, but quickly gets in a fight. Clark tells his parents he's leaving Smallville, and suggests to Lex that they team up in Metropolis. While Lex goes to find out from the Kents what's going on, a U.S. marshal turns up at the Luthor mansion searching for Jessie, interrupting Clark giving Lionel some 'advice'. Clark takes the marshal's gun away, firing bullets into his own hand to show his invulnerability, and the marshal tells him that Jessie's father has a valuable computer disc. When Clark goes to Jessie's house to get the disc, Pete exposes him to green meteor rock, weakening him so that Jonathan can destroy the red ring. Although he can apologize to his parents for his behavior, he can't explain it to Lana, and she is unforgiving. Lionel is left wondering about the three spent bullets he finds on the floor of the mansion.

MARTHA: I think our not-so-normal son might be going through some classic teenage rebellion.

JONATHAN: Well, I think I liked dealing with heat vision a lot better than that.

"I love the idea that the ring becomes a metaphor for drugs," Ken Biller says. "I think that *Smallville* is at its best when we can find a metaphor for contemporary social problems within the mythology of the show."

"The red kryptonite made Clark the wild card, which was very interesting," Al Gough adds. "When you take the center of your series and put him in that place, in a weird way you don't have a center — he becomes a moving target."

Jeph Loeb had come on board *Smallville* as consulting producer at the start of the second season. As well as being an accomplished film and television writer, he is also one of the best-known contemporary comics writers, whose tale *Superman For All Seasons* shows the young Clark Kent in a very similar light to the *Smallville* series. "The guys told me that I'd have to swim now, and shoved me in the deep end — but they gave me a pretty nice float to go with," he comments wryly. "Al and Miles knew that they

Opposite: Clark Kent, rebel without a cause.

wanted the red kryptonite in Clark's class ring. I knew that the one place that I wanted to get to was that Clark kissed Lana, and she thinks it's a real kiss. I knew that was the money. If we could get to that place, then everything else would be okay. As far as I was concerned, his head could turn into a giant ant, and it would still be okay!"

Understandably, there was some concern about turning Clark bad. "I said that if we were going to do this story, we had to embrace it," Ken Biller recalls. "It has to spiral and escalate, and get to the point where Clark is the villain of the story. I also felt very strongly that there shouldn't be a memory wipe. He should remember *exactly* what he did. He was indulging impulses that he wouldn't normally indulge, but the impulses were real. He was willing to indulge them because he was 'on drugs' — it's only because of his human upbringing and the moral code that's been instilled in him by his parents that he doesn't indulge those things."

To emphasize the red theme of the episode, production designer David Willson worked with director Jeff Woolnough to accentuate the color pallet. "In every scene there was something popping up at us," Willson notes. "There was a piece of red clothing, or red in the lighting, or in the background. The police car lights were red,

Opposite: Clark fulfils his wishes with Lana.

SMALLVILLE TORCH

Volume 52, Number 3

SEEING RED

Smallville High School students were shocked to learn this week that what were thought to be genuine rubies in their class rings were, in fact, cheap imitations made from Smallville meteor rocks... I contacted the world-renowned gemologist, and now former head of Gearhart/Nelson's Science and Gemology Division, Dr. R. K. Davis.

"The rocks are meteor rocks from Smallville. They are very similar to the more common green rocks that have littered Smallville for thirteen years. Staff members of Gearhart/Nelson discovered these new rocks near Hob's Pond during a routine green rock search and thought that they could pass for rubies, consequently allowing the company to sell a cheaper, imitation product for a higher cost."

When asked about health concerns related to the rocks and therefore the rings, Cynthia Davis dismissed them as "ridiculous" and called Dr. Hamilton's published reports on the rocks "an affront to science".

"We have been experimenting with these rocks — the green ones — for years without any problem or signs of physical effects, in spite of what Dr. Hamilton believed. They are harmless," she stated.

By Chloe Sullivan

the lights in the bar were red. We enhanced the stained glass in Lex's office to thicken up the background a bit." Jeff Woolnough adds, "We put a red filter in the camera to tint the picture. Red's the color they use in fast food restaurants to get you to eat quickly and get out, and we wanted to add to the kind of anxiety that was going on inside the character."

CLARK: Lana... I really am sorry.
LANA: I know you are. It's not enough any more.

"We expanded on the little flame effect that appears in Clark's eye for the heat vision," Mat Beck explains, "and Brian Harding made it a little devilish, hellish red flicker that happens in the iris of his eye when he puts on the red K. It's not only an effect — Tom does the facial expressions very well, and we piggyback off that."

"Tom knew exactly how to play 'Dark Clark'," Greg Beeman says. "One of our best moments in that episode is where the camera pushes a little bit closer up to him after he's beaten up all the guys in the bar and goes, 'Anybody else?'"

"There's a bad boy in all of us," Al Gough maintains, "and I think to see it in Superman really helps to humanize the character. We needed to see that he was dangerous. I remember watching the first cut of 'Red' and thinking that he was genuinely scary. Superman unleashed with no conscience would be scary as hell." ∎

DID YOU KNOW?

In original DC Comics continuity, red kryptonite was formed when some green kryptonite went through a space cloud. In the post-1986 continuity, a chunk was created by Mr. Mxyzptlk.

NOCTURNE

WRITTEN BY: Brian Peterson & Kelly Souders
DIRECTED BY: Rick Wallace

GUEST STARS: Sean Faris (Byron Moore), Richard Moll (Mr. Moore), Gwynyth Walsh (Mrs. Moore), Mitchell Kosterman (Sheriff Ethan)

DID YOU KNOW?

Metron Pharmaceuticals, the company that carried out the experiments, is named after the time-traveling DC Comics character Metron.

A mysterious admirer leaves Lana a poem on her parents' grave, but she doesn't know that its sender, Byron, is usually kept prisoner in the basement of his house by his parents. Clark is concerned that Lana is being stalked and follows her to the graveyard, where he startles Byron, making him trip. Clark and Lana take Byron back to the Talon, but he panics when he realizes it's nearly dawn, and insists on returning home. His mother tries to get him inside the house secretly, but his father discovers them, and then threatens Clark and Lana. The teenagers persuade Jonathan Kent and Sheriff Ethan to come with them to rescue Byron from abuse, but Byron's parents say he died eight years earlier, and Chloe finds his death certificate. Pete and Clark go back to Byron's house to release him from the basement. Unfortunately, as soon as sunlight hits him, he becomes a wild animal and attacks both teenagers, then goes looking for revenge. Byron's mother explains that Byron underwent medical experiments which left him in this condition, and Chloe learns that the experiments were financed by LuthorCorp. Byron goes to the mansion to attack Lionel, and grabs the helicopter in which Lionel and his new personal assistant, Martha Kent, are flying. Clark speeds to the rescue and manages to slam Byron into a darkened well, where he reverts to normal. Martha persuades Lionel to finance research into a cure.

CHLOE: Could it be that our new Shakespeare has a-stirred the heart of our young Juliet?

LANA: It's just nice to meet someone who's so honest with their feelings. I don't have to guess what they're thinking.

"'Nocturne' is another extreme version of the Clark story," Al Gough explains. "Here's a kid with a condition, whose parents literally lock him in the basement. It's an extreme parenting episode — contrasting how these parents deal with Byron, and how the Kents deal with Clark. Episodes like this and season one's 'Leech' are good because they go right to the family aspect of the show."

John Schneider thought it was "great that it was depicted first off as if these people had locked their child in the basement for no reason — but no, that wasn't the case. Those parents weren't wrong in what they were doing."

If anybody's actions are wrong in this episode in fact, it's Clark's. "He lets him out," Al Gough points out. "Clark's a teenager, and he doesn't have all the facts. He's doing what he thinks is right, but ultimately unleashes the kid, and he causes damage. Just because you have the power and you think you're in the right doesn't always mean

Opposite: Lana is entranced by Byron.

'Underneath It All' by No Doubt
'Love Song' by Sheila Nicholls
'Don't Ask Me' by OK Go
'Crazy Richie' by Cactus Groove

you're taking the right course of action."

Demonstrating Byron's powers kept the stunt department busy. "We did a fifty-five-foot chuck for 'Nocturne'," stuntman Christopher Sayour recalls. "Rehearsals were brutal for that. Clark is standing at the top of the porch of the house, and when Byron hits him, he has a wire pinned to his back. There's a crane a hundred feet high, and the wire is connected to a ratchet system, which is a hydraulic system that pulls you at great velocity. That yanks him the fifty-five-foot distance, but about twenty feet into that, they release the wire, so Clark's flying!"

The sequence where Byron attacks the helicopter provided some interesting moments for the Entity FX crew. "If the kid is catching a helicopter, you can't play that off-screen," Mat Beck says. "If you see him hanging on to a skid, then cut to a horrified facial expression, it feels like a cheat. So we CG-ed an entire helicopter, and decided that as long as we were doing that, Byron could tilt the helicopter down, and it could start chewing up a hedge. We had a separate element of a hedge being chewed up, and put that in. The actor was hanging on a crossbar that represented the skid, and we had to find a piece of his action that made the helicopter roll, so that the rotor comes toward

Below: Clark battles Byron's darker side.

camera and chops up the bushes. We couldn't track it to the exact action of his hands on the live-action footage — I guess he doesn't have a lot of experience hanging on to a Bell Jet Ranger! — so we CG-ed some hands onto the skids instead, and made the helicopter do what looked good."

The effects team also helped heighten the atmosphere in the graveyard scenes. "We added lots of fog in certain of the shots, so the whole thing had the appropriate eerie feeling and a certain amount of continuity," Beck says. "A lot of the impact of the show is emotional, and the emotions are triggered in part by a sense of the environment. If the environment is bouncing around, then it's like someone is messing with the volume while you're listening to Beethoven's Ninth!"

LEX (to LIONEL): If I find out that you have any agenda that could hurt the Kents, this amiable father-son détente will come to an abrupt end.

'Nocturne' marks the start of the Lionel/Martha relationship. "We told John and Annette that in season two we were going to start to expand the parents beyond just Clark," Al Gough recalls, "so that every scene wasn't what I would call a 'Geneva Convention on Superpowers'. We wanted to expand the lives of the adults, and introducing new relationships onto the show always gives it a new dynamic. It played into our mythology as well — you get to see what Lionel does. He's very seductive, and flatters you. When you feel underappreciated, he can step in there. It was also fun to put John and Annette in scenes together that didn't involve kids." ■

Smallville ✦ Ledger

* * * Volume 64, Number 18 * * *

WHERE THE SUN DON'T SHINE

Imagine for a moment that you never attended high school. Better yet, imagine having rarely seen the light of day, basked in the warmth of the sun or breathed the fresh air of the outdoors. Imagine that from the confines of your basement, you've learned everything you know about the world from reading books by candlelight. Such a life is difficult for most of us to comprehend. However, for sixteen-year-old Byron Moore, this is not an imaginary world; this is reality. Since the age of eight, this is how Byron has lived his life. Any exposure to the sun causes a violent reaction that makes his adrenal system launch into overdrive.

Witnesses to this occurrence say that the side effects include off-the-chart strength and extreme aggressiveness (not to mention a rather blanch complexion). For years, no one knew of Byron's existence. His parents kept him out of the sun by confining him to the dark basement of their home...

By Chloe Sullivan

REDUX

WRITTEN BY: Russel Friend
DIRECTED BY: Chris Long

GUEST STARS: Sarah-Jane Redmond (Aunt Nell), Richard Gant (Principal Reynolds), Maggie Lawson (Chrissy Parker), George Coe (William Clark)

An apparently healthy teenager sinks to the bottom of the school pool, dead from old age. His girlfriend, Chrissy, is a newcomer to Smallville High, and is keenly organizing Spirit Week. When another student is found aged to death, Chloe discovers records online that indicate that Chrissy has been alive for nearly a century. New Principal Reynolds wants to meet Chrissy's parents, so she makes him her next target. Clark intervenes, saving the principal's life. Chrissy then ages to death. Finances are tight for the Kents, but Jonathan refuses to let Martha ask her father, William Clark, for help, since he knows it will confirm in his father-in-law's eyes that he is a failure. They have been estranged for years, but Martha contacts him anyway, and Clark accidentally arrives when his grandfather is visiting the farm. He tries to make peace between the generations, but both Jonathan and William are too stubborn to change. Clark goes to visit Mr. Clark, who gives him a check. Jonathan explains that part of the reason for the rift is that they were concerned that Martha's father might expose Clark if he saw him demonstrating his powers.

Lana, meanwhile, finds a photograph showing her mother being embraced by a man who isn't Lana's father. Lex helps her identify the man, and Lana realizes that this might be her biological father.

LANA: All these years, I've had this image of the Kents as the perfect family.
CLARK: I guess we're just as dysfunctional as everyone else.

'Redux' had a checkered history, and although it kick-starts one of the underlying plotlines of the second season with Lana's discovery of the photo of her mother with Henry Small, it's not an episode which cast and crew find particularly memorable. This is essentially because, even though it was aired as the sixth episode of the second season, it was in fact shot at the very end of the first season, when everyone was exhausted from working on 'Tempest'.

"Chris Long had a great attitude about it, and did his very best," Greg Beeman recalls, "but he got the short end of the stick. He did his director's cut on it, and then halfway through the summer, just before we started back to work on the second season, we looked at it and decided that we would throw a lot of visual effects at it."

Entity FX stepped in to assist with the final cut of the episode. "We had to construct lots of things out of whole cloth," Mat Beck says. "Because the nature of what was asked for now was different from what was shot originally, we didn't have the elements that we

Opposite: Clark can't understand his father's stubborness.

DID YOU KNOW?

Martha's parents moved to Coast City, which in DC Comics continuity was the home of super hero Green Lantern. It was destroyed during the Reign of the Supermen after Superman's death at the hands of Doomsday.

needed to do stuff. We had to create some things completely. There's a sequence where Chrissy looks at her face as this mirror goes round, and Joey Brattesani did a really good job building that decay and degenerative process. It was helpful that the rotating mirror provided a bit of a slideshow, so we didn't have to make it as a complete organic, full transformation. We did it as a series of 'snapshots', each one of which was moving, which allowed us to give it some emotional impact. We re-edited the sequence a couple of times, and dropped an effect shot and added some other ones in. We also had to do a quick-decaying body with CG. Not our most elegant work," Beck admits. "I still squint when I see it!"

'Redux' does provide Smallville High with a new principal, replacing the late Principal Kwan. Although Principal Reynolds has been name-checked in a few episodes subsequently, this is his only appearance to date. "The idea was that we were going to use him, and then it just didn't work out," Al Gough explains. "When you start breaking

Smallville ⬤ Ledger

* * * Volume 64, Number 19 * * *

EZRA SMALL AND THE YEAR IT RAINED FIRE Part II

In our ongoing commemoration of Smallville History Month, here is the continuation of 'Ezra Small and the Year It Rained Fire', an account that was compiled from various source materials, including surviving fragments of Ezra Small's personal journal, currently in the McDaniel Collection at the Lowell County Historical Society, Edge City, Kansas:

Early on the morning of his encounter, as Earth's yellow sun vainly tried to cut through the winter clouds over Kansas, Ezra had found his traps empty. That wasn't too unusual for this time of year. What was noteworthy, however, was the trail of blood leading from some of them into the woods.

October had passed, and with it went the last of the homesteaders who would jokingly refer to his ramshackle assembly of mud and thatch huts as "Smallville". No other human was around to steal those beavers. Ezra wondered if he would regret his decision to stay put and continue trapping instead of joining the others at the brigade base camp.

Following the trail of blood drops in the hard-packed ground, he was soon surprised to see a group of beautiful wolves circling in front of him. Ezra had never known wolves to be interested in a dead animal from his traps, yet these certainly appeared to be likely culprits. He recalled waking in the night to several pairs of glowing eyes surrounding his tent, uncharacteristically casing the grounds restlessly. *Food must also be scarce for them,* he thought.

Brandishing his rifle, Ezra cautiously continued forward. He knew the wolves would never attack him, but their calm stares were deeply unsettling...

By Christopher James Beppo

stories, you realize there's not a lot this guy could do. There wasn't much to play there, and the character can only give you so much, so we ended up dropping him."

Above: Clark tries to build bridges between his father and grandfather.

LANA: So, where are you going to be in five years?
CLARK: In college, probably studying journalism.
LANA: You're kidding.
CLARK: Don't tell Chloe, but I think it's growing on me. I like to find the truth behind things. I'm tired of having secrets in my life.

SMALLVILLE MUSIC

'Mickey' by B*Witched
'Can I See You' by Buva
'All My Life' by Foo Fighters
'Boom, Boom, Boom'
   by The Outhere Brothers
'I Feel Fine' by The Riddlin' Kids
'Ivanka' by Imperial Teen
'Be Aggressive'
   by The Jockjam Cheerleaders
'You Ugly' by
   The Jockjam Cheerleaders
'U Girl' by Sophie Agapios
'Somewhere Out There'
   by Our Lady Peace

Gough is happier with the other introduction in the episode. "In terms of the mythology of our show, 'Redux' sets up Lana and her biological father, which was something interesting out of an otherwise tired episode." Ken Biller agrees that Lana's search for her father added a 'soap opera' feel to the show. "It's absolutely soap opera, for sure," he admits. "But the idea wasn't to do something soap opera-y. As Clark was finding out about his origins, she was finding out about hers, and trying to forge connections with the parent. And what would that be like? That was another storyline where there were several episodes where we shot three or four scenes, and by the time it was cut for time, there'd be one scene that might seem to come out of nowhere. That can be frustrating. That's just the limitations of TV. If an episode comes in at fifty-four minutes and it's got to be forty-two minutes, you end up chopping lots out, particularly character stuff that focuses on guest characters — we always keep the Clark/Lana scenes!" ∎

LINEAGE

WRITTEN BY: Kenneth Biller
STORY BY: Alfred Gough & Miles Millar
DIRECTED BY: Greg Beeman

GUEST STARS: Blair Brown (Rachel Dunleavy), Patrick Cassidy (Henry Small), Mitchell Kosterman (Sheriff Ethan), Malkolm Alberquenque (Young Clark), Matthew Munn (Young Lex)

A middle-aged woman ambushes Clark at school, claiming she is his birth mother. Rachel Dunleavy is convinced that Clark is her son Lucas, the only child adopted through Metropolis United Charities, the organization who arranged the paperwork for Clark's adoption by the Kents. She's been attracted to Smallville by Chloe's continued investigations, and when Clark learns this, he and Chloe have a major argument. However, Chloe tells Clark that Lionel Luthor founded the charity, and Clark questions his parents with this information. Jonathan explains that they needed Lionel's help to make Clark's adoption legal, which he was willing to give as thanks for helping him get Lex to the hospital in the immediate aftermath of the meteor shower. Rachel was Lionel's mistress, and she believes Clark is Lex's half-brother. She gets a court order for a DNA test, but Clark and Pete swap samples. When she learns there's no correlation, Rachel kidnaps Lex and demands that Lionel confirm Clark's parentage or she'll kill Lex. Lionel refuses, and Clark arrives just in time to save Lex. Jonathan then explains to Clark that Lionel made him persuade the Rosses to sell their factory to Lionel in return for his silence over Clark's adoption.

Lana goes to see Henry Small, the man in her mother's photo, and although he's initially hostile, he eventually agrees to take a DNA test. Lex asks Lionel about his newly-discovered half-brother, but Lionel claims he died in infancy — however, he has a photo in his locket of a much older boy...

> **CHLOE (to LANA):** You know, I could tell you where he went to college, I can tell you how many outstanding parking tickets he has... I can even pull up his dental records and let you know if he flosses regularly. But, if you really want to know who he is, I would suggest using the hi-tech research device called... the doorbell.

"I think 'Lineage' is a beautiful episode — a very lyrical story," director Greg Beeman says. "It always helps to have a great script, and on 'Lineage' I got a good card."

"'Lineage' was one of the five stories that we pitched originally," Al Gough recalls. "It was going back to see how the Kents adopted Clark. We say that *Smallville* is 'Superman with paperwork' — we wanted to understand how Clark was adopted. It's something that we wanted to do in season one, but we held it back, and it turned out really well. It finally helped put the rest of the pieces together as to why Jonathan hated

Opposite: Jonathan realizes he has made a deal with the devil.

DID YOU KNOW?

Writer Ken Biller is a veteran of genre television, co-writing the classic *X-Files* episode 'Eve', and producing and writing for *Star Trek: Voyager*.

Lionel, and explained what we set up in 'Zero', when Jonathan blew Clark off when he asked about the adoption. It also set us up for Lex's bad seed brother."

"Miles and Al knew that they always wanted to do a story about what happened the day of the meteor shower, and Clark finding out that Jonathan had made a deal with the devil to get those adoption papers," writer Ken Biller explains.

JONATHAN: Hey, since when did Martha Kent believe in magic wands?
MARTHA: Since the moment I laid eyes on this little boy.

Although a lot of the story is set in 1989, "there are only three flashbacks," Biller points out. "They're long, but there's only three." Miles Millar suggested that Beeman look at a John Sayles movie called *Lone Star*. "It tells the story of a town in Texas through some flashbacks which are very simple and elegant. The camera pans around and you're in the past."

"Once I'd grasped that concept, I got really excited about it," Beeman admits, "and I think it was a very successful effect. It's very theatrical. It all had to be very well-designed so we could move back and forth from the past to the present in camera without doing any visual effects tricks. We changed night to day in the same shot — the little boy runs over to Martha, then in the present I had the little boy hug her legs, then tilted up the camera, and it was now day. I literally yanked the little boy off camera and set Tom on camera!"

Below: Clark queries his adoption.

Mitch Kosterman had fun with the sideburns required for the 1989 Deputy Ethan. "They put these two big things which looked like two squirrels on the side of my head," he laughs, "and I asked Greg if they were okay. He said they were fine, but he confessed later that it was dark and he didn't really get a good look, so when we came to shoot the scene, he wondered what he'd approved!"

"That was a pretty straightforward episode, except for the day out in the cornfield," Mike Walls recalls. "We did it in thirteen hours — we had predesigned everything, and we shot it all in two fields to do minimal damage. We had huge fire pits set up in the center of the fields, and you can't imagine the heat out there." The destruction was increased by the visual effects team for the long shots. "The script actually said that the corn was flattened as far as the eye could see," Mat Beck explains, "but [executive producer] Ken Horton wanted to see a boundary to the region of destruction. So we ended up creating a wall of erect, untrammeled corn around our fake, trammeled stuff."

"'Lineage' feels like it's a lot about the past, but it has a very strong present-day story," Ken Biller notes. "It was important to make Rachel sympathetic and have her believe that Clark was her son. There's a great ad lib that John Glover and Blair Brown did in the office, when Lionel leans in to seduce her, and starts to kiss her, telling her how beautiful she is." ∎

SMALLVILLE MUSIC

'Yesterday' by Hef
'Otherwise' by Morcheeba
'Put It Off' by Pulse Ultra
'17 Years Down'
   by Wonderful Johnson
'Un Bel Di Vedremo' (from
   Puccini's *Madame Butterfly*)
   sung by Renata Tebaldi

Smallville 🐓 Ledger

* * * Volume 62, Number 20 * * *

METEOR SHOWER ROCKS SMALLVILLE
Residents Left Reeling After Out-of-This-World Storm

Smallville prides itself on being 'the place where nothing happens'. This week, something big changed that. These are the stories of what will surely become known as the Great Meteor Shower of 1989.

Among the Smallville landmarks damaged in the meteor shower are two popular eateries, Jane's Café and Ma's Eats, the latter of which may be irreparable. The Smallville Savings and Loan building took a direct hit to its second floor. Fortunately, several members of the Crows football team, on hand for the ill-fated parade, helped most of the employees escape injury. And the historic abandoned Creekside Foundry was pummeled to the point of becoming even more structurally unsound than it already was.

One locale that some residents may not regret seeing devastated is the site of the planned Pleasant Meadows housing project, a development being managed by an outside firm. The awarding of the contract to a Metropolis company, LuthorCorp, had been protested vigorously, but supporters of town council president Bill Tate's ambitious expansion approach prevailed.

By K. Jean Daimuzo and the *Ledger* staff

RYAN

WRITTEN BY: Philip Levens
DIRECTED BY: Terrence O'Hara

GUEST STARS: Ryan Kelley (Ryan James), William B. Davis (Mayor Tate), Sarah-Jane Redmond (Aunt Nell), Martin Cummins (Dr. Garner), Mitchell Kosterman (Sheriff Ethan)

Ryan James (see season one's 'Stray') is being held against his will in the Summerholt Neurological Institute in Metropolis, where tests are being carried out on his telepathic powers. He manages to get to a phone and calls Clark for help. Clark breaks him out and takes him to Lex's mansion. The institute's Dr. Garner calls in Sheriff Ethan, and Clark agrees to hand Ryan over the following morning. Unfortunately, Ryan's aunt gave Dr. Garner legal custody, so there is little option. Just in time, Lex arrives with a court order giving the Kents temporary custody. Ryan has been getting increasingly bad headaches, and knows from reading Dr. Garner's mind that he has a brain tumor that is killing him. Lex discovers that a Dr. Burton in Hub City specializes in such cases, but he is leaving the country. Clark races the 425 miles and persuades Dr. Burton to operate on Ryan. However, it's too late, and Ryan spends his last few days with Clark.

Meanwhile, Aunt Nell wants Lana to move to Metropolis with her and Dean, but Chloe suggests she move in with her. Lex battles Smallville's corrupt Mayor Tate, who wants a campaign contribution from Lex in return for continued favors. Lex refuses and decides to finance Tate's opponent in the next election.

RYAN: Why do you think Devilicus went bad?
LEX: I'm not sure. Probably wasn't aware of it. You see, Ryan, in life, the road to darkness is a journey, not a light switch.
RYAN: You should remember that, Lex.

"If the audience doesn't get emotionally involved with your characters, then you're dead," executive producer Bob Hargrove says bluntly. "You're going to be cancelled. The moment we forget that, the show will go. Features can get away with action and bad acting — you go one time to a movie, and then it's your decision if you want to go back and see it, or buy the DVD. With episodic television, you cannot do that. 'Ryan' was one of our absolutely best episodes. It was a wonderful piece for that terrific young actor."

"I knew that Al and Miles wanted to bring Ryan back because he was one of the favorite guest stars from season one," Ken Biller recalls. "It was another risky thing. Did we want to kill a kid on television, a kid the same age as a lot of our audience? It was about what happens when you can't save everyone, even though you're Superman with all these powers. Running really fast or being really strong isn't going to help. Our most successful episodes are where Clark has a trial, and has to learn that things aren't easy,

Opposite: Jonathan and Martha break the bad news to Clark.

SMALLVILLE MUSIC

'Pacific Coast Party'
by Smashmouth
'Tie Me Up' by Handsome Devil
'Bad Idea' by Bad Ronald
'The People That We Love' by Bush
'My Bridges Burn' by The Cult

and is then changed by it. He has to watch this young friend of his die."

"Ryan is a character that the audience knows, so there's some emotional investment in him," Al Gough points out. "It wasn't just a guy we met at the beginning of the episode. At the end you think he's going to be okay, and he's not. It's part of Clark's journey to adulthood. It's one of the things we learn — people die, and life's not always fair." "At this point in our history, we were learning that we could survive on our acting and writing as well as we could on visual effects," Greg Beeman notes.

RYAN: This moment. It's perfect. I don't want you to be angry or sad. You changed my life. You're going to change a lot of people's lives, Clark. Promise me you'll never give up?

CLARK: I promise.

Effects still had their part to play, however. Ken Horton encouraged the visual effects team to enhance Dr Garner's villainy. "At the end of the teaser, he took a needle and stuck it in Ryan's head," Horton recalls. "I told them to build me [in CG] a *massive* needle! You don't see it go in, but you see it on an angle, and clearly get the sense of it."

Below: Clark rescues Ryan from the Sommerholt Institute.

Smallville ⬤ Ledger

* * * Volume 64, Number 21 * * *

RYAN JAMES SUCCUMBS TO CANCER

Pediatric patient Ryan James died yesterday afternoon at Smallville Medical Center. James was involved in an accident last year here in Smallville and stayed with Jonathan Kent's family. He later moved to Edge City to reside with his aunt, who gave up legal guardianship and presumably left Kansas. Jonathan and Martha Kent were recently granted temporary custody of the thirteen-year-old.

James suffered from a rapidly growing brain tumor. Famed cancer researcher Dr. Thomas Burton, who developed an experimental serum that shrinks primary brain tumors, operated on the young teen and administered the serum, but the procedure came too late. Jonathan, Martha, and Clark Kent were with Ryan James when he died.

Funeral services will be held at the Kent farm on Friday, with burial immediately following at the Smallville Cemetery. In lieu of flowers, please send donations to the LuthorCorp Children's Fund.

By Kathy Romita

Meanwhile, Mat Beck and his team worked hard on what the visual effects producer describes as "the superspeed extravaganza". "We manipulate time a lot," Beck explains. "We speed it up, slow it down — and do it within one shot, which gives a certain energy. In 'Ryan', Clark zooms up to camera and suddenly everything slows down. You can tell that, because suddenly some leaves that were blown around by his passage are suspended in the air, and birds that were flying by in the background hang in the air, and Clark is running at normal speed. We're seeing super-fast, then we cut to a reverse shot, and we see the back of the leaf that we just saw the front of in the previous shot start moving, and Clark has disappeared. We put some blur on him, and distorted the background a bit. I guess the actual physics of it would be a little different — but hey, in terms of telling the story, it works pretty good!"

The only physical effect was for the sequence at the end when Ryan and Clark go floating over Smallville in a balloon. "We created the balloon basket on stage," David Willson recalls. "We did quite an exhaustive search on finding a nice *Smallville*-colored balloon which fit our pallet. We did air-to-air filming with a helicopter and the balloon over the fields, and at the same time shot plates that we could use to marry to a greenscreen, hanging the basket from our ceiling on the stage."

"Every week our show is a little bit different," Greg Beeman says. "It was one of our cheapest ever episodes, with a very strong script, and I think it is one of our most heart-tugging stories." ∎

DID YOU KNOW?

Although most people think of 'Rogue' as the first time that *Smallville* visits Metropolis, 'Jitters' actually has that honor — Jonathan and Martha head there for their wedding anniversary.

DICHOTIC

WRITTEN BY: Mark Verheiden
DIRECTED BY: Craig Zisk

GUEST STARS: Jonathan Taylor Thomas (Ian Randall), Robert Wisden (Gabe Sullivan), Emmanuelle Vaugier (Dr. Helen Bryce)

Clark's classmate Ian Randall is furious when he learns that he is going to get a C in metal shop. The teacher refuses to change his mark, and is horrified when two Ians menace him, one of whom stabs him. Chloe and Lana have moved in together, but are both attracted to Ian, and he uses his ability to create a second version of himself to enable him to date them both. When Clark and Pete find the teacher's body, they are nearly killed by one of the Ians, while the other creates an alibi with Chloe. Clark and Pete set a trap for Ian, with both seeing an Ian at the same moment, but Ian thinks that the girls were responsible, and the two of him kidnap Chloe and Lana from the *Torch* office, taking the girls to a dam to kill them. Clark saves both his friends as one Ian falls to his death.

Lex is sent to anger management classes, where he meets up with Dr. Helen Bryce, who he once encountered in Metropolis. They eventually agree to date. Jonathan has an accident on the farm, and Martha feels guilty that she wasn't there to help because of her job with Lionel. She offers to resign, but Jonathan admits he needs to come to terms with her job.

CHLOE: You really can't imagine that someone would choose me over Lana, can you, Clark?

"'Dichotic' had an interesting genesis," Ken Biller recalls. "The idea came up about doing a krypto-villain who could split himself in half. Mark Verheiden and I did a whole story about a guy who was a reporter for a television station, and he used his powers to split himself so that he could both create a news story and tape it at the same time. The original teaser was that he shoved somebody out a window, and you saw the body plummet, and at the same time saw the same guy videotaping it and getting a scoop. He'd come to Smallville to get a story — the assassination of Lex Luthor. He'd kill him and tape it at the same time. But we decided to make it more high school based. It became a metaphor on trying to super-achieve at high school."

"It was a Freak of the Week episode that put a kink in the triangle of our existing characters," Al Gough notes. "It really blew open the whole Lana-Chloe-Clark dynamic. I loved the last scene where Clark tells them to bugger off and then leaves, as opposed to them sweetly making up!"

"The problem of any ongoing story is that on the one hand we want the characters we're familiar with, and on the other, you have to search for ways to change them up," Greg Beeman comments. "What if one guy could have both Chloe *and* Lana? I thought Jonathan Taylor Thomas was very strong in 'Dichotic'. I'd never seen that dark side to

Opposite: The doubly charming Ian Randall.

him — I thought he was like a young Val Kilmer."

All involved with the production are in awe of Kristin Kreuk's willingness to swing hundreds of feet over a dam. "It's unnerving to the best of stunt people, because you're basically just on a wire," Christopher Sayour points out. David Willson adds, "Kristin just hung over the edge of the dam, which is about a four or five hundred feet drop. She's a real trouper — and it saved us all kinds of money not to have to recreate that with greenscreens and stunt doubles."

CHLOE: So, what do we do now?

CLARK: Well, first we can stop treating me like the jealous boyfriend, since none of us have actually dated. You want to be friends, let's be friends.

It still involved the Entity FX team in work, though. "That's an example of an effect that no one particularly recognizes," Mat Beck says. "We had to do an enormous amount of wire removal, using the computer. Everyone was wired within an inch of their lives — I think the dam could have collapsed and they would still have been fine! It's one of those trade-offs: you have the reality of the person in that environment, but at the same time we had to do a lot of wire removal, including patching over bits of the talent themselves."

Smallville Ledger

* * * Volume 64, Number 22 * * *

FORE! LEX LUTHOR GOES BERSERK

Moments after being issued a parking citation, Lex Luthor grabbed his nine-iron golf club and violently attacked the parking officer's car, smashing the windshield and the taillights.

"Apparently, Luthor thought he was being targeted by me and just snapped," said Officer Pete O'Grady. "I've never seen someone go so crazy over a parking ticket. It's not like he can't afford to pay it."

Fortunately for Luthor, he did not strike the officer during his unscheduled 'golf practice', or he would have certainly been arrested and charged with a felony. The volatile millionaire was additionally cited for vandalism of a city-owned vehicle and now has to pay a much larger fine and attend court-ordered anger management classes.

Words of advice, Lex: stick to the fairway.

By Angie Perez

Beck and his crew used three different techniques to create Ian's unique splitting ability. "We built a CG back, and a CG face pushing through it in 3-D," he explains, "and then we played it almost like a shadowplay for another shot, which by definition is in 2-D. When they finish separating, the strands that go 'boing' and snap were generated in 2-D."

Originally both Ians died. "They both fell off the dam, and we shot that," Mark Verheiden recalls. "It ended with them reaching out and touching each other, with their fingers fusing a little bit, and then they died. But Jonathan Taylor Thomas was so good that we decided to keep him around…" ∎

Above: Chloe falls for the wrong guy (again).

SKINWALKER

WRITTEN BY: Brian Peterson
& Kelly Souders
STORY BY: Mark Warshaw
DIRECTED BY: Marita Grabiak

GUEST STARS: Patrick Cassidy (Henry Small),
Tamara Feldman (Kyla Willowbrook), Gordon Tootoosis
(Joseph Willowbrook), Mitchell Kosterman (Sheriff Ethan)

Local Native American leader Joseph Willowbrook is furious that LuthorCorp is building an office park on his tribe's sacred lands. Shortly afterward there is a major explosion at the site, witnessed by a white wolf. Clark falls into a cave where he meets Kyla Willowbrook, Joseph's granddaughter. Old paintings on the walls depict the prowess of Naman, a man from the stars who has superstrength and can shoot fire from his eyes. Clark also spots an indentation the same shape as the spaceship key. Clark and Kyla are increasingly attracted to each other, particularly after Clark saves her life in a rock fall in the caves and she believes he is Naman. They try various methods to persuade LuthorCorp to stop the work. When Lex sees the key indentation, he too takes an interest in the caves, eventually arranging for the state to take responsibility, with LexCorp in charge of the work. It emerges that Kyla's tribe were known as skinwalkers, since exposure to green stones allowed them to change into animals. A white wolf attacks Martha as she leaves work, then stalks Lionel in the mansion before Clark comes to his aid. The wolf is fatally injured, and turns back into Kyla, who dies in Clark's arms.

Meanwhile, DNA tests confirm that Henry Small is Lana's father, but her joy is muted when she learns that Whitney is missing in action.

KYLA: It was prophesied that Naman would fall from the skies in a rain of fire. They say that Naman will have the strength of ten men and will be able to start fires with his eyes.

"We'll take a good idea from anybody," executive producer Al Gough maintains. "From a writer's assistant to the network executive that gives us notes. We are always open to good ideas."

The story for 'Skinwalker' was written by Mark Warshaw, who is responsible for *Smallville*'s internet presence, heading up, with Chris Freyer, the team who write the articles for the *Ledger* and *Torch* that interweave with the show's ongoing story. "Mark had this idea and showed me an outline he'd written about a Native American girl who fell in love with Clark," Ken Biller recalls. "The central idea was that she was going to help reveal Clark's destiny to him. We bought the story from Mark, and gave it to Kelly and Brian to write. It introduced the caves, and opened up our mythology. It delved into Clark's origins, and he finds out that maybe people from his planet had been to Earth before, giving him some connection to the tribe." "It starts to lay the

Opposite: The entrancing Kyla Willowbrook in the Kawatche Caves.

SKINWALKER

seeds that Clark wasn't sent here by happenstance, which gets played out more later," Al Gough teases.

'Skinwalker' introduced the Kawatche caves, which fill a stage at the *Smallville* studios in Vancouver. "We had one space we could stick it into, so we maxed it out as big as we could get," production designer David Willson explains. "It was a one-shot deal, that we thought was just scripted as almost a throwaway. We found a real cave location that might have worked, but we realized that we could get more mileage out of it if we had it standing on stage. We always enter it by a different end, and exit from the side, and use moveable pieces which make it look several times bigger than it is. One of the challenges was trying to figure out a cave that would fit into Kansas' geology. It's sandstone, almost like an abandoned subterranean riverbed, which worked well because we could leave the ceiling open."

Working with wolves, or even the wolf/dog cross that played the wolf in 'Skinwalker', is always challenging. "It had to jump through glass," David Willson says. "We couldn't find a pure wolf that could act that wouldn't chew any actors up!"

"One of the hardest morphs we ever had to do was where the wolf changes into the girl at the end," visual effects supervisor John Wash recalls. "They both have faces, but you can't imagine how different they are. A wolf is mainly snout with a minor mouth

Smallville ● Ledger

★ ★ ★ Volume 64, Number 23 ★ ★ ★

HIDDEN TREASURE FOUND IN SMALLVILLE

A series of cryptic cave paintings thought to be over 500 years old have been discovered underneath the former site of the proposed LuthorCorp Corporate Plaza. The paintings are thought to have been drawn by the Kawatche tribe, among the earliest settlers of the Smallville area.

Professor Joseph Willowbrook of the Central Kansas A & M Center for Indigenous Nations Studies — a full-blooded Kawatche — was instrumental in saving the caves from destruction. Willowbrook, who had been searching for this particular set of drawings for "[his] entire life", explained that, "These paintings tell the most important Kawatche legend of all, the legend of Naman."

According to Willowbrook, Naman was to come to Earth on the wings of an eagle and have the strength of ten men. "He's about 500 years late," conceded the professor/activist. "But that is not the point. These caves are a link to my ancestors. Our history around these parts precedes Ezra Small's settlement by centuries. Kawatches were here way before that fur trapper. Of course, there is no statue of the first Kawatche in front of Smallville's City Hall."

By George 'The Streak' Talmer

hanging!" "Morphs are almost like some psychological perceptual test," Mat Beck adds. "In going from one face to another, you come up with all these intermediate stages that are very *interesting*. Halfway between a beautiful wolf and a beautiful girl there was an ugly girl, so we tweaked the morph so that she stayed attractive. There was a moment where she had really nice eyes and a dog nose!"

CLARK: Lex, have you ever wondered if you were destined to be with someone?

LEX: You're asking someone who's been fighting his destiny his entire life.

A change in the storyline also meant some extra work for Entity FX. "The shot of the wolf watching at the start of the episode grew in complexity," Beck explains. "For storytelling purposes, it was decided that the wolf would watch the actual explosion, whereas it had been filmed as if it was watching just the aftermath of the explosion. We had to light the wolf up differently, so we recomposed it, shrunk things down, steadied the picture and put the wolf in place. Then we hid the head of the trainer, who was hiding beneath the wolf's feet, and did a lot of color correction. It ended up looking as if the wolf was really sitting in front of the explosion." ■

SMALLVILLE MUSIC

'Outtatheway' by The Vines
'Don't Know Why' by Norah Jones
'The Game of Love' by Santana
featuring Michelle Branch
'Psycho Ballerina' by Jackpot

VISAGE

WRITTEN BY: Todd Slavkin
& Darren Swimmer
DIRECTED BY: Bill Gereghty

GUEST STARS: Eric Johnson (Whitney Fordman),
Lizzy Caplan (Tina Greer), Emmanuelle Vaugier
(Dr. Helen Bryce)

DID YOU KNOW?

A *Smallville* fan gave Eric Johnson a version of the *Saving Private Ryan* poster retitled 'Saving Private Fordman', which now hangs in the *Smallville* production office in Vancouver.

A month has gone by since Whitney was reported missing in action, and Lana is amazed when he arrives back at Smallville High. He's anxious to pick up where they left off, but has no memory of her breaking off their relationship (see 'Heat'). Clark reluctantly attends a homecoming party for Whitney, but is attacked by the Marine, who seems insanely jealous of Clark. The next day, Whitney bludgeons to death a Marine lieutenant who has arrived with bad news for his mother. Clark goes to Whitney's house, where his X-ray vision reveals the same skeletal deformity that Tina Greer (from season one's 'X-Ray') had. He realizes that 'Whitney' is in fact Tina, even though Tina supposedly committed suicide the previous week. Tina interrogates Mrs. Fordman for information about Whitney, then uses Lana's kryptonite necklace to incapacitate Clark, throwing him in the storm cellar. The spaceship unexpectedly comes to life, neutralizing the necklace. Clark goes to Lana's aid and finds Tina masquerading as him. The two 'Clarks' battle and the fight climaxes with Tina's death. Mrs. Fordman then confirms that Whitney was killed in action.

Lex discovers that Helen has received $100,000 from Lionel, and eventually listens to her explanation that it was a bribe to leave Lex. He asks her to help save him from becoming his father.

LANA: The thing with Whitney is that what you see is what you get. You know, no mysteries, no deep dark secrets.
CHLOE: Unlike someone we know.

"We were thinking of killing Whitney off at the end of season one, but thought it wasn't such a good idea, and liked the notion of him going off to war," Al Gough comments. "But then in season two we didn't want to have Whitney hanging out there. We also liked Tina Greer, the morphing girl from 'X-Ray', so we combined the two story lines. You actually see Whitney die in the teaser, but you don't know he's dead until the end, *after* you've gone through all this. I think 'Visage' plays on the great horror-thriller idea that 'evil comes into your life at your weakest moments'."

The return of Lizzy Caplan was great in theory; however, as Greg Beeman points out, "it was quite frustrating because she wasn't available as she was a regular on a sitcom, *The Pitts*. We shot the whole episode without her, and then two weeks later went back and shot all of her scenes in two days." Despite the logistical problem, "it was a very satisfying episode," Beeman feels. "It had mythology, it had Whitney and answered the questions about him, and it was also a twisted lesbian love story in a funny way. There

Opposite: Whitney, home from battle
– or is he?

DID YOU KNOW?

Gary Jules' haunting version of the Tears For Fears song 'Mad World', heard in 'Visage', also featured in the movie *Donnie Darko*, and was a number one hit in Great Britain.

was the weird subtext of Tina taking over Whitney's body, wanting to marry Lana and live with her forever as a man, as well as lusting over Chloe, that I thought was funny."

'Visage' relies to an extent on knowing who these season one characters are, which concerned Ken Biller: "Was it too 'inside'? Even though the exposition was given, did it depend too much on the audience remembering who this guest character was from the previous season? But I thought it was a really cool story. Was Whitney screwed up because of something that happened to him in battle, or because of something else? It was a very powerful send off for Eric."

LANA: Did someone put something in the Smallville water supply, because everyone's acting really strange today.

The opening sequence, in which Whitney is trying to lead his troops out of danger, was filmed in Pitt Meadows, in the Fraser Valley east of Vancouver. "We found some mountains that looked like Indonesia, with a foggy background and the swampy

Below: A spark between Lex and Dr. Helen Bryce.

headwaters of the river," David Willson recalls. "That Indochina sequence took forever to shoot," Mike Walls adds. "We kept going back because we kept losing the location due to water problems, and in November there's only six hours of daylight. It was a lot of fun when we shot it."

"Cold, but a lot of fun," Eric Johnson agrees, remembering the effort that went into making the scene. "We actually went back to do some close-ups only eight days before the episode aired! It ended up looking like a piece of *Band of Brothers* or *Saving Private Ryan*. It's amazing — you put on all that equipment, and we had the real stuff, and all of a sudden you feel invincible."

The climactic fight sequence also went through numerous changes. "I think there were nine or ten action beats in that sequence originally," Mike Walls recalls, "but only about five made it to the screen. It turned into a twenty minute fight sequence — Titan versus Titan."

"We don't hold anything back," says Greg Beeman. "Our scary stuff we do *X-Files* scary; if it's a love scene, it's really gooshy; if it's a fight, it's good and violent!"

"That was a really great night," Christopher Sayour, Tom Welling's stunt double, adds. "Basically Tom and I were switching wardrobes all night. I was slamming him into things, and we were like two football players. It wasn't two stunt guys going at it — that was all Tom." ■

MUSIC

'Days Go By (Acoustic)'
by Dirty Vegas
'The Anthem' by Good Charlotte
'Mad World' by Michael Andrews
featuring Gary Jules
'Love' by Rosey

Smallville ⊛ Ledger

★ ★ ★ Volume 65, Number 1 ★ ★ ★

FAVORITE SON PERISHES IN WAR
But Mysteries Abound

It had been a while since Smallville had any reason for fanfare until Private Whitney Fordman, having been officially listed as missing in action in Central Asia, came home... or so we thought. As 'Welcome Home' banners replaced yellow ribbons, a bizarre Martin Guerre-esque plot unfolded. The person we slapped on the back, shook hands with and hugged so tight as to cut off his breath was not the same man who, as a towheaded little boy, used to run the aisles of his father's store or, as a talented high school athlete, led the Crows football team to a state championship.

So who was this impostor? And why deceive a mother, a girlfriend, an entire town? We may never truly know why, but the who — former Smallville resident Tina Greer — is just as baffling. Is this the same Tina Greer who supposedly died in a hospital fire? Friends of the *real* Whitney claim the pretender to be Greer and admit that the truth is stranger than science fiction... even for Smallville. Authorities have re-opened their investigation into the fire, and DNA testing is underway on both 'Tina Greers'.

Meanwhile, the tragedy continues for Betty Fordman, who remains unavailable for comment.

By Gena McGuiness

INSURGENCE

WRITTEN BY: Jeph Loeb
& Kenneth Biller
DIRECTED BY: James Marshall

GUEST STARS: Colin Cunningham (Nicky), Patrick Cassidy (Henry Small), Kevin Gage (Pyne), Byron Mann (Kern)

Lex discovers Lionel has been bugging his office, beating him out of a contract. His plans to return the favor go awry when he learns that Lionel has decided to make Martha work on a Sunday at the Metropolis LuthorCorp office. Jonathan isn't pleased either, as it's the Kents' anniversary. The crooks Lex hires to bug Lionel's office have a different agenda, and take Lionel and Martha hostage before plundering the offices. Lex, Jonathan, and Clark all head for Metropolis, where Clark looks for a way to sneak into the building. Lex tries to negotiate with the crooks without revealing his identity. When Martha's life is directly threatened, Clark conquers his fear of heights and leaps from the roof of the Daily Planet building onto the LuthorCorp tower, where he comes to his mother's aid. While the crooks are raiding the office, they discover a safe full of meteor rocks, and Martha also sees a file on Clark and the key to the spaceship. She pockets the key, later hiding it in a flour jar in the storm cellar, and gets Clark to incinerate the file. In the commotion caused by Clark's arrival, Lionel shoots the crooks' leader, and after they are all freed, tells Lex that he will be moving back to Metropolis. Martha wants to stop working for Lionel, but Jonathan thinks it would be better to have someone monitoring what he is doing.

LANA: What do you call your newly-discovered biological father's wife?
CLARK: Well, personally, I'd call her Mrs. Small, but that's just me.

"We got back from Thanksgiving break, and Miles came into the writers' room and said, 'I think it's time for Clark to leap a tall building,'" Jeph Loeb recalls. "We had been trying to figure out how to do a siege or a hostage situation story, and when Miles said that, we said, 'Why don't we do our version of *Die Hard?*'"

Smallville's homage to the classic Bruce Willis action movie is "one of the proudest moments in my TV career," Loeb's co-writer Ken Biller claims. "Sometimes you write a script and it doesn't come out as well as you imagine, and this is one of those rare instances where it comes out way better. It was brilliantly directed by James Marshall."

"We'd done a hostage story in 'Jitters' in season one," Al Gough says, "and then upped the stakes by setting this one in LuthorCorp Plaza. We also introduced the Daily Planet building to showcase Clark's first leap. We wrote 'Insurgence' before 'Visage' and 'Suspect', but it was shot after those, because we had to figure out how to produce it."

"Ken Biller started talking about the story in terms of *The Conversation*," Loeb continues, referencing the paranoia-filled Francis Ford Coppola film, "and shifting the focus from Clark to make it a Lex/Lionel story, which Clark is drawn into the middle of."

Opposite: Lana and her father, Henry Small.

As one of the comic book writers, Loeb was pleased at the opportunity to bring another 'real' character into the series, with the introduction of Superman's Metropolis Police Department ally, Lieutenant Maggie Sawyer. "Ken had written a hard-bitten, crusty kind of cop. I asked him if he minded if it was a woman, and explained who Maggie Sawyer was and the role she would play in the future."

LEX: Mr. Kent, ever since the day I moved to Smallville, I've done nothing but try to be a friend to you. And in return, you do nothing but lecture me with sanctimonious platitudes. I'm done listening to them.

One of the most stunning moments from the episode is Clark's leap. "We were committed to the glass and steel and blue wash of color as our look in Metropolis," Greg Beeman explains, "and we found a brand new building in Vancouver, that hadn't been occupied at the time, to be LuthorCorp. Ironically, it was adjacent to the Marine Building, which is an art deco structure from the 1930s, which Miles and Al had always intended to be the Daily Planet building."

Mat Beck and his crew took those elements and created the background for the leap. "We built a reflection map of Metropolis: all the buildings are synthetic. This composite city is a combination of CG buildings, matte paintings, and real elements from the streets, and we then reflected that in the *Daily Planet* globe. The camera flew

Below: The LuthorCorp offices.

over that, down past some blurring lights, to see Clark walk out of the roof access door onto the roof of the building."

Clark then takes a run-up and leaps across to the LuthorCorp building, crashing into one of the glass windows as he arrives. "We had Tom attached to a parallelogram in the studio," Mike Walls continues, "and he ran off the end of a piece that we'd built on the greenscreen stage, then floated in midair as he went over the sill and then started his trajectory down. That gave the CG guys all the angles, and then we filmed Tom's stunt double sliding into a sheet of glass which exploded as he hit it."

The Entity FX team then manipulated the timing of elements of the live action, speeding them up and slowing them right down to increase the effect of the leap. They swung the camera around Clark to give a sense of vertigo, as well as adding his reflection just before he made contact with the LuthorCorp building. "Tying his actions together was one of the big challenges for that sequence," Mat Beck recalls. "Compositor Eli Jarra tweaked Tom's body a little bit to give it better continuity — with this leap, the body language is what you're looking at, so we had to match all those different views." (It was worth all the effort: the shot later won a prestigious Visual Effects Society Award.)

"'Insurgence' was kicking on all cylinders," Al Gough concludes. "But it was tough to get produced!" ∎

DID YOU KNOW?

As originally created by Jerry Siegel and Joe Shuster, Superman couldn't fly — his power was limited to leaping tall buildings in a single bound.

Smallville 🐓 Ledger

* * * Volume 65, Number 2 * * *

METROPOLIS HOSTAGE CRISIS HITS HOME
Lionel Luthor, Assistant Held Hostage

A break-in occurred Sunday afternoon at the LuthorCorp Tower in Metropolis. Four armed perpetrators identified as Nicky Taylor, Jessica Bishop, Dave Kern, and Earl Pyne seized control of the corporate headquarters, holding Lionel Luthor and his assistant, Martha Kent, hostage until nightfall.

During the tense standoff that lasted over five hours, Kern and Pyne were killed, perhaps during a scuffle when power was cut to the tower. Bishop and Taylor surrendered to authorities without further incident. Sources close to the investigation report that the teenage son of Martha Kent played a key role in the rescue, but Mrs. Kent refused to comment.

When questioned about the valuables inside his safe, Luthor responded, "My confidential files and property are of no concern to anyone. What's of greater consequence is that these criminals were stopped dead in their tracks, and my assistant and I were unharmed."

By Angie Perez

SUSPECT

WRITTEN BY: Mark Verheiden & Philip Levens

DIRECTED BY: Kenneth Biller

GUEST STARS: Mitchell Kosterman (Sheriff Ethan), Jason Connery (Dominic Santori), Patrick Cassidy (Henry Small)

DID YOU KNOW?

At one stage, Gough and Millar considered making Dominic Santori the villain of the piece, but decided Sheriff Ethan should take the fall, allowing Dominic to live to fight another day!

Lionel Luthor's evening is interrupted by an unknown assailant who shoots him twice. Later that night, Jonathan Kent is woken from a stupor in his truck, clutching a bottle and a gun, and is arrested by Sheriff Ethan. Jonathan claims he only had half a beer at the Wild Coyote bar, then passed out. Lana tells Clark and the sheriff that she overheard a furious argument between Jonathan and Lionel about a watch that Luthor had given Martha, which is found in pieces at the Kent farm. Clark and Pete visit the Wild Coyote, where the bartender tells them that Jonathan was drinking heavily, and the case against Jonathan deteriorates further when gunshot residue is found on his hands. However, Clark finds a bullet embedded in a shed near where Jonathan was arrested. Lionel's aide, Dominic Santori, tells the sheriff that Lex and his father were arguing over Lionel buying up shares in LexCorp. Pete and Clark are run off the road and their car is blown up, which makes Lex believe Clark must be onto something. Clark and Pete return to the bar, but find the bartender dead. Clark sees a picture on the wall which reveals the murderer's identity to him. They set a trap in Lionel's room and catch Sheriff Ethan, who admits he framed Jonathan and shot Lionel because he hates what the Luthors stand for. When he recovers, Lionel tells Lex that he wants his son back by his side.

JONATHAN: Martha, I am so sorry.

MARTHA: For what?

JONATHAN: I'm sorry for not having faith in us. I'm sorry for giving in to my own petty fears. And all it takes is one reckless moment to ruin everything.

"I didn't want Ethan to be the bad guy!" John Schneider admits. "I liked the way 'Suspect' was put together, and thought it was a very interesting-looking show, but I would have preferred it to be somebody else because I miss Mitch. He did a great job."

"We're not a 'cracking the mystery' show," Al Gough says, "but one day I said, 'Well, what if we *did* do a mystery? What would it be?' It's a totally different episode for us, and I think it came out really well. I hate it when these stories cheat, and I don't think we did."

Once again the Japanese film *Rashomon*, with its different narrators telling their versions of the same events, was an inspiration. "We didn't know if we could do it until it was finally written," co-writer Philip Levens recalls. "It was out of the mold." Mark

Opposite: The prime suspect.

Verheiden agrees: "It's a bit of a change-around for the show. As writer, I thought picking Sheriff Ethan as the ultimate villain was really cool, because I don't think *anybody* guessed that he would be the one. I wish the ultimate reveal of him were a little bigger, though."

"Okay, it couldn't be any of our series regulars," Greg Beeman reasons, "so we had to pull a red herring out and make it Ethan. No-one was more distressed than Mitchell, because he was nearly a series regular, and just as he was feeling happy and comfortable to be part of *Smallville*, we 'killed him off'."

"I cried because I knew I was leaving the show," Mitchell Kosterman admits. "I had a hard time justifying why my character would do that when I read the original script. In that version, I took a nurse hostage against Clark — what in my character had shown me to be an evil person that I would hold a gun to a nurse's head? I was much more happy with the second version we shot. I was still a sympathetic character. I was just pushed to a bad place, and that whole dynamic of good people being pushed to do the wrong thing by bad people like Lionel Luthor is a pervading theme in the whole show."

'Suspect' marked Ken Biller's début as director on *Smallville*, and presented him with the challenge of creating flashbacks. "I wanted to do them differently from 'Lineage'," he recalls. "Along with director of photography Glen Winter, I decided to shoot everything in the present in a rather formal way, on a dolly. There were no handheld or steadycam shots in the present. The past was all shot handheld, on 16mm

Smallville ❀ Ledger

* * * Volume 65, Number 3 * * *

SMALLVILLE SHOCKED BY SHERIFF'S ARREST
Not-So-Usual Suspects Questioned

Lionel Luthor was found lying in a pool of blood in the library of his mansion by one of his live-in maids. Shot in the abdomen and just below the left shoulder by an unknown assailant, Luthor was rushed in critical condition to Smallville Medical Center, where doctors are hopeful that he will make a full recovery following surgery…

In a shocking turn of events, Smallville's esteemed Sheriff Ethan Miller has been arrested for the murder of a bartender whose body was found in the back room of the Wild Coyote, and the attempted murder of Lionel Luthor.

Several questions remain unanswered in the continuing investigation: Did Sheriff Ethan betray not only his former friend and classmate Jonathan Kent but an entire town that recently honored him? What dark motive could a trusted and dedicated lawman have for wanting Luthor dead?

By Angie Perez

color reversal film stock, which gave it that very grainy, dirty look. It gives those past sections an interesting quality."

Above: Sheriff Ethan frames Jonathan for attempted murder.

CLARK (to LEX): You grow up with someone, you think you know them, but... I mean, darkness like that just doesn't come out of nowhere.

The episode also firmly turned its focus to the older generation on the series. "Jonathan was the lead, which was unusual," Greg Beeman points out. Ken Biller adds, "John Schneider had a lot to do in that episode, and he did a fantastic job."

The scenes at the start weren't really filmed in the pouring rain, but many of the actors would probably have preferred to brave a thunderstorm than the rain towers used. "A rain machine doesn't produce ordinary rain," Mitchell Kosterman explains. "You may as well have a firehose pointed at your face. It was much worse on John than me, because I had a hat on. He would open his mouth to say something and all you'd hear was a gargle. To top it all off, they had a giant fan pointing at us as well! When we finished, there was a knock on my trailer door, and John Schneider had brought some very fine scotch to warm us up!" ■

RUSH

WRITTEN BY: Todd Slavkin & Darren Swimmer DIRECTED BY: Rick Rosenthal	GUEST STAR: Rob LaBelle (Dr. Fredrick Walden)

Pete attends an illicit rave at the Kawatche caves and is bitten by a parasite which removes his inhibitions. Lex hires Dr. Frederick Walden to translate the inscriptions in the caves after seeing Clark reading his book. Two other attendees at the rave die with enlarged adrenal glands and strange bite marks, and when Chloe and Clark go to the caves to investigate, Chloe is bitten. Dr. Walden finds a nest of alien worms, and tells Lex that the inscriptions are not human. Walden demands that everyone be banned from the caves. Chloe lusts after Clark, and he reciprocates after Pete slips him a piece of red meteor rock. Clark demonstrates his powers to Chloe, and they make out at the Talon in full view of Lana. Clark recovers his senses when the red rock falls from his pocket, so Pete uses a piece of green rock to knock him out. A bucket of water from Lana wakes Clark in time to prevent Pete and Chloe from recklessly killing themselves. The worms are removed, and neither teenager can remember anything. Since Clark wasn't infected by a worm, he can't explain his behavior to Lana. Lex tells Walden that he believes Clark knows something about the caves, and he wants him allowed free access.

CHLOE: I'm nothing more to you than your own personal search engine and I'm sick of it. I want you, Clark.

"'Rush' is a 'reefer madness' story," Al Gough maintains. "We went from 'Insurgence' and 'Suspect', which were very adult, to 'Rush', which was much more of a teenage episode. We were trying to expand the mythology of the caves, and establish the idea that the Kryptonians had put things in there that were protections and safeguards."

'Rush' also saw the return of red kryptonite. "After 'Red' did very well, the network said that they wanted another red K episode," Al Gough says, "and we said we weren't going to do another one, because 'Clark turns bad' — and then what do you do? It wasn't in any context. We knew what happened when he did it. Then we thought, 'What if a friend slips something in your drink and you don't know it?' So we told the network we'd give them one act of red K, not an entire episode."

"Allison got to be sexy, and I know she had fun doing that," Greg Beeman adds. "What was fun for me was when Red K Clark and kryptonite Chloe got together. You could see the difference. When Clark and Lana get together, it's more romantic. When Clark and Chloe get together, it's hotter!" Gough agrees: "It was fun to see Clark and Chloe making out. And once again Lana and Clark go one step forward and two steps back."

Opposite: Clark tries to bring Pete back down to earth.

Filming the sequence in which Clark catches Chloe and Pete's car — as they try to get the ultimate rush jumping the gorge — required hanging the car from a crane, something that Sam Jones III didn't exactly enjoy. "He looked like he was petrified that day!" Mike Walls recalls. "Allison was having the time of her life — although she was a little nervous in the car. She told me that once she started getting into the scene, it left her mind, but it never left Sam's mind once. As soon as we were done, we heard, 'Ah, can I get down please?'"

There wasn't even really a gorge there — the other side was created digitally. "The challenge on that was trying to find the right place," production designer David Willson explains. "We have all kinds of mountains around here, but not many cliffs. We ended up going to an old rock quarry and shot the cliff from one angle, then flipped the camera and shot it again before adding the car in."

CHLOE: Oh, my God. This is so cool. Can you fly?
CLARK: Whoa, wait a minute. I may be an alien, but I'm not a cartoon.

"We shot the car 'drop' in reverse [lifting it up and then playing the footage backwards]," Mike Walls continues. "We tried doing it in straight time, so the car would drop and stop on its own, but it didn't work that way, so I went back to the drawing board and did another test, which I showed to the director."

Smallville ⬤ Ledger

* * * Volume 65, Number 4 * * *

NOTED LINGUIST STUDYING CAVES

Lending credence to suspicions that the caves under town possess more significance than the public may be aware of, world-renowned linguist and cryptographer Fredrick Walden has interrupted his demanding schedule to reside in Smallville for a brief period while studying and hopefully deciphering mysterious carvings and symbols on the cave walls.

One of the most highly paid and sought-after experts on language, Professor Walden was on his way to Chile to study inscriptions in the Miladon Cave, but he diverted his travels upon learning of cave administrator Lex Luthor's discoveries in the Smallville caverns.

"Normally, I would not have shuffled my schedule for such a mundane locale as Smallville — no offense intended — but what I'm seeing down there is truly intriguing, and it virtually cries out for a person of my expertise and intellect to bring it to light. I was glad to offer my services to Mr. Luthor."

By Jim 'Slim' Bradlee

"We added movement to the shot to give it a little bit of reality," Mat Beck adds. "But the oddest thing is there's one shot, where the car is coming toward the camera, that looks like a bad composite. The sky is really blue, and the car just doesn't look like it belongs there. But it's not a composite — it was a real shot of the car hanging on the crane!"

'Rush' marked Rob LaBelle's début on the show. "Walden was a fun character," he recalls. "They said they wanted him to be scruffy and have a disdain for people, without a lot of formality." ∎

Above: Clark and Pete arrive at the Kawatche Cave rave.

PRODIGAL

WRITTEN BY: Brian Peterson
& Kelly Souders
DIRECTED BY: Greg Beeman

GUEST STAR: Paul Wasilewski (Lucas Luthor)

Lex saves his younger brother Lucas from death at the hands of a Chinese gang in Edge City and brings him back to Smallville, introducing him to their father. Now that Lucas is eighteen, he has voting rights under the LuthorCorp rules, and both Lex and Lionel want to use him in their power struggle. Lionel freezes Lex's assets, and Lucas throws him out of the mansion, leaving Lex to beg shelter from the Kents. They agree, and Lex throws himself into the work on the farm. Lucas realizes that Lionel is faking his blindness. When Chloe discovers that Lucas' adoption papers suddenly surfaced at the Metropolis adoption charity, Lex realizes that he has been set up. Lucas interferes with operations at the Talon, where Clark has taken up a job as a waiter, but Clark saves Lucas from being shot by one of the gangsters from Edge City, who dies in police custody. Lucas knocks Lex out, takes him to the LuthorCorp offices, and summons Lionel. Lucas wants Lionel to kill Lex himself, but he refuses. Clark has followed Lionel to Metropolis and secretly uses his heat vision to disable Lucas' gun. Lionel tries to shoot Lucas, but the gun is loaded with blanks, as is Lucas'. It was a plan by Lionel's sons to reveal Lionel's duplicity. Lionel ends up giving Lex back his company in exchange for his silence. Clark loses his job at the Talon after disappearing one too many times.

LIONEL: That's a very keen observation.
LEX: Especially from someone you told me was dead.

"'Prodigal' was an interesting parlor game with the Luthors," Al Gough says dryly. "The strength of that episode is the machinations with the Luthors — John Glover and Michael Rosenbaum are great."

"When you have John and Michael in most of your episode, you know you're in pretty good shape," director Greg Beeman says. "I know that I'm going to direct the season opener and ender, and they'll be big episodes where I get more money. But in the middle of the season, the hand gets dealt and you don't know what cards you'll be given. I knew with 'Prodigal' that I was going to have dynamic performances."

Beeman admits that he had problems following the machinations of the Luthors as Lucas switched sides with dizzying regularity. "I don't think I ever understood what Lex and Lucas' plan was to defeat Lionel," he says. "In that big scene in the end, I did a lot of shuffling photographically to keep the audience's mind off it. I used long lenses with the camera moving and drifting, which added a tension and edginess."

The director worked closely with visual effects producer Mat Beck to create the

Opposite: The new kid in town – Lucas Luthor, heir to millions?

DID YOU KNOW?

Lex's time on a ranch before the death of his mother, to which he refers in this episode, is shown in the story 'Vows' by Clint Carpenter in issue 3 of the *Smallville* comic.

scene in the alleyway where Clark rescues Lucas from being shot by the thug on a motorcycle. "'We've already had him leap tall buildings,'" Beck recalls Beeman saying, "'and now he's faster than a speeding bullet.' We had a conference to design a sequence that would tell the story in a reduced number of shots. We came up with a shot where the camera was leading Clark, so we see him running toward camera, which would allow us to show the bullets he was catching up on. Then the camera keeps going and we see Lucas, and when the shot was completed, we had Lucas, the bullets, Clark, and behind him the motorcycle with the guy, flying out of frame."

Beck found it a challenging sequence because "we needed to explain to people what was going on. Those bullets were going to kill Lucas, and Clark was outrunning them one by one. The last one he barely gets to, and he jumps on Lucas. We 'cheated' when it came to the length of the alley — in terms of how much time he really had, we would have needed four of those alleys! We also made the bullets a little bigger than real nine-millimeter bullets, so they showed up a little better. We also did all the calculations of how fast an Uzi fires, and the muzzle velocity. We figured the bullets would be twenty to thirty feet apart, so we took some liberties. We also added an insert of a leather jacket and a hand coming in to deflect the bullet at the end, which Ken Horton asked for to make it really clear that the last bullet is deflected away. Our lead compositor, Eli Jarra, really kicked butt on this job!"

Smallville 🐔 Ledger

* * * Volume 65, Number 5 * * *

LUTHOR REGAINS SIGHT

In a press conference held Wednesday morning, billionaire Lionel Luthor announced a near medical miracle — the LuthorCorp Chairman and CEO has regained his eyesight.

In a dramatic display, the eccentric businessman removed his dark glasses and proceeded to describe a journalist seated at the rear of the conference room — right down to the detailed design of her sweater. After a brief moment of stunned silence, reporters fought to be heard above the barrage of questions that riddled the room.

Luthor quieted the crowd and spoke of his restored vision: "Though my eyesight was gone, I was determined to forge ahead. Several doctors told me there was no hope. Ladies and gentlemen, there is no hope *only* where there is no will. After my recent medical emergency, I started an amazing treatment called hyperbaric oxygenation. Today I stand before you a sighted man with a clear vision of the future, and I am grateful to the brilliant doctors at the Metropolis Neurological Center."

By Shelby Taylor
Reprinted from *The Daily Planet*

Opposite: Debating a spot of patricide - Lex and Lucas unite against Lionel.

CLARK: As long as I live, I don't think I'm ever going to understand your family.

LEX: Neither will I. Just remember, my father may try and rule the world, but yours will inherit the earth.

For Greg Beeman, the episode is also notable for "the moment I noticed Tom Welling become a leader behind the scenes as well as being the lead of the show, which is the best thing for a series. If the series lead is a selfish, self-involved person, it really is a disaster. We ran out of time shooting the basketball scene when Lucas comes in and plays with Clark and Pete. I had an hour and a half to shoot the scene, and Tom just stepped up. He pulled the actors together, and told them what he was going to do, and in a matter of ten minutes he had choreographed the whole scene. Tom was almost like a quarterback on the fly, making it up. Even as director, I wasn't in a position to make that scene happen in the timeframe unless Tom did exactly what he did. He might already have become it, but that was the moment when I *noticed* Tom become the leader behind the scenes."

Kristen Kreuk remembers another aspect of her leading man: "Tom and Allison had to serve coffee at the Talon. I'm a klutz," she laughs, "but they were *terrible*. Coffee spilt everywhere, and it made me feel a lot better!" ■

FEVER

WRITTEN BY: Matthew Okumura
DIRECTED BY: Bill Gereghty

GUEST STARS: Emmanuelle Vaugier (Dr. Helen Bryce),
Michael David Simms (Dr. Neil Moore)

When Martha goes to bury the ship key, she disturbs some meteor-infected pollen that causes her to collapse unconscious. Jonathan is amazed when the subsequent medical examination reveals that Martha is pregnant, since the Kents had been told that they cannot have children. The Kent men are alarmed when the Center for Disease Control arrives to investigate, and Clark and Pete race to the farm to remove the ship before it is found. Clark is also affected by the pollen in the process, and eventually collapses into a fever. To Jonathan's amazement, Helen Bryce is able to take a blood sample from Clark, and he begs her to check the sample herself. While Clark is drifting in and out of consciousness, Chloe pours out her feelings to him, but is devastated when he calls her Lana. Jonathan breaks into the C.D.C. to retrieve the ship key, since hopefully the ship can save Martha, and although he's still unwell, Clark helps him. Pete decoys the C.D.C. away while Jonathan and Clark take the ship to the hospital, arriving just after Helen has declared Martha dead. The ship activates and sends out a pulse that revives Martha.

Lex invites Helen to move into the mansion with him after he learns that she has been offered a chance to go to Johns Hopkins and leave Smallville.

CLARK: Pete, are you sure the ship will be safe in your shed?
PETE: Yeah, we'll put it between the old Betamax and my dad's Pong game. Indiana Jones couldn't find it down there.

"The problem with Superman is that the guy can do anything," Ken Biller points out. "So how do you put obstacles in his way? I think it was interesting to see Clark vulnerable like he is in 'Fever'. It's also the first time that Clark's secret gets revealed to someone totally outside. The Kents have always said that they can't take Clark to a doctor. And in this case, in desperation, they choose to trust Helen Bryce, and give her access to Clark's unique physiology."

"This is where we plugged Helen into the mythology of the series," Al Gough adds. "She has Clark's blood, and what would that mean?" Emmanuelle Vaugier found that particular scene one of her most difficult on the entire series. "It was more frustrating than challenging in many ways," she explains. "I had to tie the rubber band around his arm, and the needle was there strategically placed so that I could pull the fake vial of blood that was hidden underneath Tom's arm, so that it looked like I'd actually drawn blood. It all had to get done within a certain time frame before the conversation with Mr. Kent. It was the last scene of the day, and I just *couldn't* get it! I've done scenes like that before, but that day I just couldn't do it right. I was relieved when I saw it, because

Opposite: Clark and Jonathan try to help the fevered Martha.

DID YOU KNOW?

Writer Matthew Okumura is one of the production staff based at *Smallville*'s Los Angeles head-quarters, working for executive producers Alfred Gough and Miles Millar.

at least it looked like I knew what I was doing!"

"Allison has a beautiful scene that was reworked a lot by the writers," Greg Beeman recalls. "It was a scene that she was quite anxious about, and wanted to do really well. It's quite touching and opens up her character a lot. I asked Miles and Al to apply their special touch to that scene — it was a really important moment, which had a lot of potential to be corny and really fail. It was a monolog, which is really hard for an actor to pull off. And they went back to the global theme — everybody wears a mask, the theme of secret identities. Allison is a really strong actress, and it's easy for her to do a good job when she's got good words."

The sequence in which the meteor-affected pollen enters Martha's lungs took Entity FX into *CSI: Crime Scene Investigation* territory, with the camera moving 'inside' a human body. "Did we really want to sculpt the alveoli of the lungs?" Mat Beck remembers debating. "We wanted to honor a certain amount of anatomy, but take certain liberties to make it look cool. We choreographed it so that we're flying along

Opposite: Chloe opens her heart to an unconscious Clark.

Smallville ☙ Ledger

* * * Volume 65, Number 6 * * *

MEDICAL CENTER MIRACLE!
Mysterious Light Accompanies Patient's Sudden Recovery

After her heart monitor flatlined and revival efforts seemed to have failed, Smallville resident Martha Kent was pronounced dead at 2:17 a.m. yesterday morning due to a respiratory infection. But at approximately 2:20 a.m., Mrs. Kent mysteriously started to breathe on her own, and the inactive line on her monitor started to beep with life.

Attending physician Dr. Helen Bryce had attempted to resuscitate Mrs. Kent when the patient's heart stopped moments earlier, but the doctor failed to get a response. "I pronounced the patient dead," Dr. Bryce said, "and the nurses and I began to clear the equipment. Then the room got very bright, and Mrs. Kent's revival followed."

Interim Sheriff Mark 'Wink' Waid said the Sheriff's Department would investigate the reports of a bright light, but he feels there is a logical explanation. "It was obviously a power surge or maybe a spot from one of the helicopters the Disease Control Agency's been flying around town," Sheriff Waid said. "Nothing to worry about, folks."

By Brice Robinson

with the little green particles, but they're also moving in camera as well. It's a combination of exposition and geography — this is what's happening and this is where we are — and as we move around this little hillock of lung tissue, we see all the little alveoli in the distance turning green."

CHLOE: I may not be the one you love today, but I'll let you go for now, hoping one day you'll fly back to me because I think you're worth the wait.

The effects team also had to do one of what Mat Beck describes as their "invisible" effects. "We added the message on the Talon marquee," he says. "They pushed in on the sign with no letters on it, and then we composited the letters on to it. We don't do that every time, just occasionally when there's been no time to do it practically, or it needs to change."

"'Fever' had a really strong dramatic idea behind it," Al Gough says. "What if the authorities investigate the Kent farm? This place that's always been very private is suddenly having every nook and cranny looked into. It was a nightmare scenario for the Kents: Clark sick, Martha dying, and people swarming all over the farm trying to figure out what's wrong, and they've got to hide the secret. With all that, you're bound to come up with a really good episode." ▪

SMALLVILLE MUSIC

'Wave Goodbye' by Steadman
'Not That Simple' by Jamestowne

ROSETTA

WRITTEN BY: Alfred Gough
& Miles Millar
DIRECTED BY: James Marshall

GUEST STARS: Christopher Reeve (Dr. Virgil Swann),
Rob LaBelle (Dr. Frederick Walden)

As Lex gives Dr. Walden a three-day deadline to translate the strange cave symbols, Clark is drawn to the spaceship key, which he inserts in the cave wall. A stream of light hits him, downloading information. Clark wakes to find Lex and Walden wanting answers. The next day, Clark involuntarily sears a burning symbol into the Kents' barn wall with his heat vision. Chloe puts it on her website, attracting the attention of New York-based billionaire recluse Virgil Swann. After he retrieves a piece of paper on which Clark has doodled the symbols, Lex orders Walden to work with Clark. Instead, Walden returns to the cave and inserts the key in the slot. It floods him with a different sort of light, leaving him catatonic. Swann e-mails Clark another symbol, which Clark can now translate as 'I'm a friend'. Despite his parents' concerns, Clark travels to New York to meet the billionaire. Swann informs Clark that he received messages from Krypton at the time of the meteor shower asking him to protect and keep the infant Clark, whose real name is Kal-El, from evil. A second message for Clark says, 'We will be with you, Kal-El, for all the days of your life.' Clark learns that Krypton itself no longer exists, and there are no others like him on Earth. Clark returns home and inserts the key in the ship, which informs him of his special destiny to rule Earth, although Jonathan comforts Clark, telling him that his human upbringing will ensure he remains a good man.

> **CLARK: Lex, why do you care so much about an old Native American language?**
>
> **LEX: Because I don't think it's Native American. I don't even think it's from this planet.**
>
> **CLARK: You think aliens wrote it? I'd keep that to yourself, Lex.**

"'Rosetta' was the high point of the season," Al Gough states. "We had always wanted Christopher Reeve to guest star in the show — it's something that we'd been thinking of since the pilot — and I called his agent and asked if he would even consider doing it. We found out that he'd watched the show, and thought it was very well done. When we were arcing out the second season, we knew we had this character who was going to tell Clark where he's from and where he's going, and we wanted Christopher Reeve to play him. It's the passing of the torch. Obviously hearing that Clark is from Krypton and that the planet blew up is news to no one but Clark, so we wanted to find a way that could be dramatic. It's not just some backfill about his past — there's a

Opposite: Dr. Virgil Swann.

ROSETTA

cautionary tale about Krypton. Is it so hard to believe that a bright race could destroy their own planet? We spoke to Chris, who's really a fantastic guy, and he liked the idea of the character, and then it was a logistical chessboard in terms of how we were going to do this."

Because Reeve was confined to a wheelchair, and required numerous helpers when he traveled, the decision was taken to film his scenes in New York, nearer to his home. "We had a lot of lead time on that segment," producer Bob Hargrove recalls. "It was easier to send Greg Beeman there to shoot his scenes. James Marshall was directing the episode in Vancouver, and we sent Greg to New York."

Al Gough, Tom Welling, Greg Beeman and visual effects supervisor Mat Beck worked with Christopher Reeve on location. "John Wells has always been very good to us," Al Gough notes, "and he very generously let us use the production offices from *Third Watch* to shoot the scene. We redressed a couple of rooms, brought Chris in, did a press conference, he shot for ten hours, never leaving the set, and then we shot a public service announcement at the end. The next day he got on a plane for Australia!"

"The moment when Tom and Chris met each other was amazing," Greg Beeman says. "Christopher Reeve was a gentleman. We had a long scene, five or six pages, which is usually enough to cover a twelve hour day. I was told at first we had three to four hours to shoot, because Chris didn't have enough endurance to go beyond that. I was quite intimidated by that, so I staged the scene very simplistically. I had Tom in front of Chris, and then he made one move behind. Chris said that it wasn't going to work — Tom had to move around him or there would be no dynamics to the scene. As he said quite correctly, 'Tom moving around me will hide the fact that I'm unable to move.' We re-blocked it with that idea in mind, and it was much better, but on a mathematical level, it added a lot of shots. I went up to him and said, 'This is great, but there's a lot more to shoot, and I've been told that you can only shoot for four hours.' He said, 'Oh, no — this scene has to be great. It doesn't matter how long I'm here. Let's do it!'"

"It was fun to see Christopher Reeve working," Mat Beck recalls. "He was thinking like an actor and also like a director. It was a cool little symbolic moment where the older Superman is acting with the newest."

CLARK: 'On this third planet from this star Sol, you will be a god among men. They are a flawed race. Rule them with strength, my son. That is where your greatness lies.' I think I was sent here to conquer. What kind of planet am I from?

Opposite: Clark and Dr. Swann, face to face.

"There was so much weight to the environment that day," Tom Welling says, "with the scene and meeting Christopher for the first time. It was a really amazing experience for me personally, on a professional level to work with Chris, and on a character level to get all that information. It was an *amazing* day." ■

Superman Speaks
Christopher Reeve on the day of filming

"I was a little bit skeptical when I heard about it at first, but I must say the writing, the acting, and the special effects are quite remarkable. In 1977 a big stunt scene would have taken us a week to film — it's pretty impressive what they are able to do with computers and effects technology today on a weekly TV show. It gives it a lot more production value and inventiveness than I thought I was going to see when I first heard about the series. I think the show is doing a really good job following the mythology, and Tom is doing a good job following the tradition.

"I thought it would be fun; it's a very welcome relief from politics and medical research. Butting heads with politicians and the whole establishment in terms of advancing medical research is a very difficult job, and time-consuming and energy-consuming, and this is a very welcome change of pace.

"I read the last page of the scene, and the door seems to be open [for me to return]... let's see how I do on this one first. If I bomb on this one, that'll be the end of it!"

VISITOR

WRITTEN BY: Philip Levens
& Michael Green
DIRECTED BY: Rick Rosenthal

GUEST STARS: Emmanuelle Vaugier (Dr. Helen Bryce),
Jeremy Lelliot (Cyrus Krupp)

Clark starts to believe that new student Cyrus Krupp may also be an alien when he seems to use heat vision against class bully Kyle and his gang. Cyrus tells Clark that he arrived on Earth on the day of the meteor shower, and is building a transmitter to contact his people. Lana's horse Tyson is now boarding at the Kent farm and falls sick, but Cyrus is able to heal it. Chloe reveals that Cyrus' 'heat vision' was simply the use of magnesium strips, but that doesn't explain the healing. Clark helps Cyrus retrieve his electronics project, which had been confiscated after the heat vision incident. However, Cyrus is taken away by Child Protection and Clark busts him out of Smallville General. Chloe discovers that Cyrus' parents were killed during the meteor shower. Cyrus has built a massive transmitter tower in the woods, but the bullies try to destroy it. Clark attempts to stop them, but as a light descends from the sky, a chain breaks Kyle's neck. Although he believes he'll lose his last chance to leave Earth, Cyrus uses his power to heal Kyle, but the exertion sends him into a coma.

Meanwhile, Helen Bryce finds a room in the mansion that her master key won't open. Lex eventually reveals a room dedicated to understanding his car accident and investigating the Kents. Helen is torn because, over Jonathan's objections, Martha is now her patient.

**CHLOE: Can you imagine being from another planet? The experiences you
could share?**
CLARK: It wouldn't freak you out?
CHLOE: Compared to most people, I think aliens would be a step up.

"'Visitor' started from the notion of what would happen if somebody showed up and Clark began to believe that he wasn't the last person from his planet." Ken Biller says. "It might be wishful thinking on his part, but this person really might be from Krypton. Society would think that this person was crazy and a freak, but he might not be." "It took the information we had learned in 'Rosetta' and moves it on," Al Gough adds.

The story went through various changes to make the parallels between Clark and Cyrus more pronounced. "It seemed a bit incredible to me that a kid would think that he might need to scare off some bad guys, so he would rig an explosion and then make it look like he'd shot fire out of his eyes in order to scare them," Ken Biller notes. "I always believed it was enough for Clark to say, 'Who knows what people are like where I come from — they could all have different powers.'"

Opposite: Clark wonders if he really is the last survivor of Krypton.

'The Other Side' by David Gray
'Kiss the Moon' by Hathaway
'Phantasmagoria In Two'
by Neil Halstead
'Wartime' by Stephanie Simon
'Diamonds and Guns'
by Transplants

Contrary to what might be expected, the tower that Cyrus builds in the woods was a practical, functioning set. "'Visitor' had one of our best sets ever," Al Gough comments. "David Willson is such a wonderful production designer."

Willson's inspiration came from working on a "film in North Carolina called *Love Field*, with Denzel Washington and Michelle Pfeiffer," he recalls. "We ran across an old man called Bowler Simpson. His daughter had perished in a car accident on the way home one night, so old Bowler decided to make this giant, kinetic art piece of sculpture, made out of license plates and STOP signs. Over about twenty years, he turned this ten-acre field into a memorial. I took that image and used it for the tower. It actually tipped over within twenty degrees of the ground, and all the little pieces rolled around and jiggled and jangled. We drew it to a certain extent, but then we all just jumped out there and put the pieces on."

"It was a big build for this show," Mike Walls adds. "We buried it under the ground, and had it all on a hinge so we could control it down to the minutest detail. I'd figured

SMALLVILLE TORCH

Volume 51, Number 16

BURNING QUESTION: ALIENS OR ARSONISTS?

Are aliens invading Smallville? Or are arsonists just intent on burning it down? Earlier this week, an unidentified symbol was emblazoned into the side of Jonathan and Martha Kent's barn, and it has left more questions than answers.

If arson, this would be the third attack on the Kent farm in the last year. Last fall, several canisters of LuthorCorp toxic waste were dumped on Kent grazing land—killing several head of their cattle. And in May, the Kents' truck inexplicably exploded.

Not surprisingly, this barn-burning incident, too, has left local authorities stumped.

"It's very difficult to burn with such precision. There are no traces of magnesium powder strips, which are usually used for such pranks. We are a bit baffled," Smallville fireman Roy Gage said.

Some speculate that this may not be the work of pranksters at all. One eyewitness compared the symbol to those found in crop circles. Crop circles have long been associated with extraterrestrials, believed to be messages—or warnings—from another world.

Do aliens now find crop circles passé? Smallville is ground zero for meteorites — why not aliens as well?

City officials, not surprisingly, refused to comment on such speculations. But Sheriff Waid offered a message to any potential copycat prankster.

"Arson is a felony. This ain't 'T.P.ing' a house or chucking water balloons at cars on Loeb Bridge Road," Waid said. "The Kents could've lost their barn, and when the perpetrators are caught, they're gonna see themselves some jail time."

By Chloe Sullivan

Above: Cyrus atop his transmitter tower.

out over the course of the show that there are certain things to fight for. To do certain gags absolutely the right way means going big on them, and doing them feature film-style, and that was one of them. It made sense to do it that way because it saved them time shooting, and it gave the director everything in terms of what he wanted."

CYRUS: You're not meant for this Earth any more than I am. I'll take you back to your real home.

CLARK: This is my real home. Everything I care about is on Earth. Good luck, Cyrus.

The tower was enhanced by Entity FX's 2-D department. "We didn't do much in this episode," Mat Beck recalls, in contrast to 'Rosetta', which had been a major job for the team with its flying dream sequence and the light beams coming from the Kawatche cave walls. "We had beams coming out of the tower, and the trick was to make them look like they were in three dimensional space. But by this time, we'd been working on the show long enough to make energy beams pretty straightforward!"

"Jeremy Lelliot did a nice job, and he was very empathetic at the end of the day," Greg Beeman says. "He gave a very haunted performance," Al Gough adds. "I think there's some good emotion in that episode." ■

DID YOU KNOW?

The musical jingle that accompanies the Millar Gough Ink logo at the end of each episode was composed by Mark Snow.

PRECIPICE

WRITTEN BY: Clint Carpenter
DIRECTED BY: Thomas J. Wright

GUEST STARS: Michael Adamthwaite (Andrew Connors), Emmanuelle Vaugier (Dr. Helen Bryce), Camille Mitchell (Sheriff Nancy Adams), Anson Mount (Paul Hayden)

Clark is arrested by new Sheriff Nancy Adams after he warns off three frat boys who have been harassing Lana, throwing one of them, Andy Connors, onto the hood of a police car. He has to serve forty hours of community service, but Connors takes out a million-dollar lawsuit in damages. Lex offers to teach Lana some self-defense, and when Clark tells her that he knows that Connors is faking his injury, Lana makes Connors reveal he is uninjured, then kicks him to the floor.

Meanwhile Paul Hayden, an old boyfriend of Helen Bryce, has arrived in Smallville. In the Talon he disappears before talking to her, but then brings flowers to the hospital were she works. He and Lex have an instant mutual dislike, which is fuelled when Helen's car won't start and Hayden offers Helen a lift. Lex warns Hayden off, but the man deliberately hurts himself and claims Lex beat him up. Hayden later viciously attacks Helen in the hospital. Clark and Lex track Hayden down to the station, where the two older men fight. Lex draws back from shooting Hayden at the last moment, and later tells Helen that he couldn't kill him because she would have known the truth, even if he'd claimed self-defense. He then proposes to her.

ADAMS: I ran a complete check on your son, Mr. Kent. He's been at more crime scenes than Eliot Ness.

MARTHA: If Clark's been involved with police business, it's only because he was trying to help people.

ADAMS: Or maybe he's got some kind of hero complex? I mean, even heroes got to play by the rules.

"'Precipice' is a case where I think the script was pretty good, and the episode itself turned out excellent," enthuses Al Gough. "Tom Wright did a great job directing it. If you were dubious about the Lex/Helen relationship, I think this is the episode where you really understood why these two people were together. It's our darkest episode of the second season, and it's great. It's beautifully shot, and goes to the darker corners of the show, which are fun to explore. Emmanuelle does a really good job as Helen Bryce — she fits into our world really well, and I think she and Michael have a really good chemistry that you can just sense. You can write the best scene in the world, but if the actors don't have any chemistry, you're never going to get the magic."

By this stage, the writers had decided on Helen's ultimate path. "Our intention

Opposite: The dark side beckons to Lex.

initially was to kill her off by the end of the season," Gough reveals. "But we didn't, because Emmanuelle was so good, and we knew we could do more with her. Initially she was going to die on the wedding day, but we thought there was some more mythology to be played. The idea that she had Clark's blood sample made her very interesting, not just in terms of her relationship with Lex, but also with the Kents. The fun thing about television is that you keep peeling away the layers and telling these stories. You have the ability to go, 'This is a good character — let's try this.' You always have to know where you're going, but you can't be afraid to turn down a couple of side roads, because you never know what delights you are going to stumble upon. Emmanuelle is definitely one of the delights."

LANA: You've been there for me so many times. I wanted to repay you. Besides, it's not every day that Lana Lang gets a chance to save Clark Kent.

"'Precipice' was the right marriage of director and material," Greg Beeman comments. "Tom Wright came from *The X-Files* and *Millennium*, and a lot of dark shows, and it was only by coincidence that he got this script, but it was perfect because it was very dark, eerie and creepy."

Below: Lex brings out Lana's 'hidden dragon'.

"When you do an episode about Lex, it ends up being darker in general," Ken Biller agrees. "There were some concerns about the violence. When Hayden smashes himself in the mirror to make it look like Lex beat him up, there was a real close shot that was all bloody. It was really the moment when you realize that he's completely nuts, and after the fact we noticed the similarity to the moment in the first *Dirty Harry* film [when the killer claims he has been assaulted by Harry Callaghan]. We talked about him hiring someone to beat him up, but that would have been a direct reference. We thought it would be more interesting if he was talking to someone, and we think he's talking to Helen, but then we reveal he's actually talking to himself in the mirror."

"I remember lying down in a huge pool of blood," Emmanuelle Vaugier says of the aftermath of Helen's beating at Hayden's hands. "It was freezing! We were inside, but I was on a cold linoleum floor in my lab coat and a skirt and little top. I think they used a tighter shot in the final episode."

There was a lighter moment on the streets of Cloverdale when John Wash set up the shot of Clark seeing Andy Connors removing his neck brace inside the car. "We built up apple boxes for the actors to sit on, which would match the height of their seats in the SUV," he recalls. "We shot them doing their reference action on these apple boxes without any car around them at all. We didn't need the car — we just needed their activity to sell the X-ray effect. There was a crowd out wondering why these guys were sitting on boxes pretending to be carousing in the middle of the street!" ∎

SMALLVILLE MUSIC

'Becoming' by Adam Tenenbaum
'Don't Fear the Reaper' by Gus
'Princess' by Matt Nathanson
'Don't Forget Me'
    by Red Hot Chili Peppers
'Let Me Be the One'
    by Sammi Morelli
'Shakedown!' by TheSTART

Smallville 🐓 Ledger

* * * Volume 65, Number 9 * * *

DYNAMIC DUO:
Heroes or Vigilantes?

Two of Smallville's very own were involved in a near deadly drama that culminated at the train station last night. Lex Luthor and high school student Clark Kent were questioned by new Sheriff Nancy Adams at the scene where the two made a daring citizen's arrest of suspect Paul Hayden...

"These two gentlemen were very lucky not to have gotten hurt. The Smallville Sheriff's Department is well-trained and equipped to handle these situations. We advise the public not to take the law into their own hands," urged Sheriff Adams. "Smallville doesn't need vigilantes on its streets."

... With the increase of violent crime in Lowell County, many young women are turning to martial arts and self-defense classes to feel more secure about their personal safety.

By Angie Perez

WITNESS

WRITTEN BY: Michael Green & Mark Verheiden
STORY BY: Greg Walker
DIRECTED BY: Terrence O'Hara

GUEST STARS: Camille Mitchell (Sheriff Nancy Adams), Zachery Ty Bryan (Eric Marsh), Patrick Cassidy (Henry Small)

Clark tries to stop a truck hijack, but discovers the three robbers have strength equal to his own. They take a trunk from the truck, and Clark notices that one of the robbers has a metal plate in his head, which he later spots at school in rising baseball star Eric Marsh. Clark sees Marsh use a green inhaler, and follows him to the Smallville Foundry, where the robbers are melting down and inhaling the refined kryptonite bars they stole from Lionel Luthor's truck. They try to kill Clark by tossing him in the furnace, but he escapes and anonymously tips off Sheriff Adams about Eric, who is then arrested. Lex wants to know what was in the LuthorCorp truck, and bails Eric out, much to Clark's annoyance. Eric attacks the Kents, and Clark persuades his parents to leave town. Lex and Clark agree to set a trap for the trio, but Clark deliberately springs the trap early, and defeats them using his heat vision and superspeed. He then asks Pete to bury the kryptonite in the woods.

Lana's relationship with Henry Small is threatening his wife Jennifer, who tells Lana she is contemplating divorce. Lana tells Henry that he should stay away from her until he has resolved his marital problems.

After falling out badly with Clark over his unreliability, Chloe meets with Lionel Luthor. The *Torch*'s offices are destroyed, and Lionel then offers Chloe the opportunity of a column in the *Daily Planet*, as well as a grant to repair the *Torch*. Lionel claims he is interested in the odd events around Smallville.

CHLOE: There is no 'we' any more Clark! There's only me! And this paper was my whole life! It was the one place I could come to when everyone and everything let me down, and now I don't even have that anymore.

"We certainly know how to sell the sizzle," Al Gough laughs, referring to the memorable trailers for 'Witness', which prominently featured Clark's naked backside as he escapes from the blast furnace.

"'Witness' went through a real long gestation," Ken Biller notes. "The original idea, and why it was called 'Witness', was that Clark witnessed a crime. It was similar to the one that was in the final episode, but his problem became, how can I come forward and say I witnessed this crime? How can I explain to the police that I was standing out in the middle of the road with no car or anything at two o'clock in the morning? It was a super hero problem — getting the bad guys without revealing his identity. He made an anonymous tip, and it built to a moment in the courtroom which was about whether

Opposite: Clark tries to take the law into his own hands.

Above: The seduction of the
innocent begins.

Clark was going to testify or not. But the story kept changing, and became an episode about three guys with kryptonite poisoning who can beat up Clark. There are some good emotional moments in it, like Clark realizing that he can't protect his parents, and trying to keep them away."

No one seems to have much respect for the villains. "They have the strength to hurt Clark's parents, but they're not using their strength in a particularly bright way," comments writer Mark Verheiden. "It's like 'Rogue', without the brains!"

The sequence in the blast furnace was filmed in "an old warehouse that had nothing in it," David Willson recalls. "Everything has to be bigger than life on *Smallville*, so we made a blast furnace that was about forty feet square and thirty feet tall. We'd found an old incinerator that was about 100 feet in diameter and 200 feet tall, and fallen in love with it. It had a big center core and I was going to build the blast furnace in there, but then we found out it was toxic, so we couldn't use it. We ended up building this monstrous rusted old hulk of a blast furnace instead."

Of course, neither Tom Welling nor his double were actually put in a flaming furnace. "It was a dramatic scene with a high camera, and there were a lot of reflective elements," Mat Beck explains. "In order to make it real, there was a lot of painting of reflections in the door and the floor to make it look like he really was in a flaming environment."

'Witness' saw the new sheriff start to flex her muscles. "Sheriff Ethan's departure gave us the opportunity to introduce a new sheriff who's a cross between Holly Hunter and the sheriff in *Fargo*," Al Gough says of Camille Mitchell's Sheriff Adams. "I really like her," Ken Biller adds. "She's a lot of fun and brings a breath of fresh air to the show.

DID YOU KNOW?

John Schneider's favorite action super heroes when he was growing up were Courageous Cat and Minute Mouse. Michael Rosenbaum nominates Flash Gordon, as played by Sam Jones in the 1980 movie.

She's a very idiosyncratic character, which I like a lot, and we'll continue to use her."

The episode also saw the start of the relationship between Chloe and Lionel Luthor. The first episode of the short internet-based *The Chloe Chronicles* (see page 154) debuted on AOL the same night as 'Witness' aired, and saw Chloe investigate the aftermath of the death of Earl Jenkins, the hostage-taking janitor from 'Jitters' — a trail that leads her toward LuthorCorp. "I was very excited when I found out there was going to be a juicy arc with Chloe and Lionel," John Glover says. "Allison's work on the show fascinates me and I figured I'd be able to learn a lot from her. She's still 'forming' as an actor — not restricted by a lot of rules — and I'm trying to figure out how to break a lot of 'rules' I've learned over the years. We have a blast working together. She's got a great sense of humor, too."

JONATHAN: I want you to remember something, son. They have your strength, but they don't have any of your other abilities. You make sure you give yourself a fighting chance.

"We revved up the whole Chloe and Lionel story in this episode," Mark Verheiden recalls. "I thought that worked extremely well, even though overall it's not one of my own favorites." ∎

Smallville ⊛ Ledger

* * * Volume 65, Number 10 * * *

SMALLVILLE HIGH NEWSPAPER DESTROYED

The office of Smallville High School's controversial student newspaper, the *Torch*, was recently wrecked by a senseless act of extreme vandalism. No one was hurt during the incident, but the paper's computers, files and furniture were completely smashed by unknown assailants.

Under the editorship of sophomore Chloe Sullivan, the *Torch* had become known for its muckraking investigations of local figures as well as its almost single-minded focus on unexplained phenomena in the area. Thanks to her work at the paper, Sullivan had even landed a prestigious internship at the *Daily Planet* in Metropolis last summer.

In an unexpected act of charity, the LuthorCorp Foundation, run by business titan Lionel Luthor, announced that it was making a donation to Smallville High with funds earmarked specifically toward rebuilding its journalism department. "LuthorCorp is dedicated to helping our youth fulfill their potential," said the company's director of public relations, Mitchell Taylor.

According to Sullivan, a new issue of the *Torch* is already in the works, proving once again that stopping the presses is easier said than done.

By Frank Moore

ACCELERATE

WRITTEN BY: Brian Peterson & Kelly Souders
STORY BY: Todd Slavkin & Darren Swimmer
DIRECTED BY: James Marshall

GUEST STARS: Camille Mitchell (Sheriff Nancy Adams), Neil Flynn (Pete Dinsmore), Jodelle Micah Ferland (Emily Eve Dinsmore)

Lana believes she is being haunted by the ghost of her childhood friend Emily Dinsmore, who drowned six years earlier. Emily's father tells Clark and Lana that she is definitely dead, but once they leave, he tells his clearly alive daughter not to see Lana any more. However, she superspeeds away after injuring her father. Clark confirms that Emily's skeleton is in her coffin, but then he and Pete see her in the graveyard. Clark superspeeds after her but she disappears. Clark and Lana break into the Dinsmore's house and find Emily's bedroom in the basement, as well as a laboratory containing glass tubes with live clones of Emily inside, fuelled by kryptonite. However, when Clark gets the sheriff to investigate, she finds there's nothing there. Clark eventually tracks Emily to the abandoned house. She realizes she's not the 'real' Emily, but runs off when Lex turns up. They compare notes and realize that Lionel is using cloning scientist Dinsmore to make kryptonite-enhanced clones of his daughter. Emily persuades Lana to come with her to the river where she died, as Dinsmore tells Lex that the clones have no conscience. Emily tries to drown Lana, but Clark arrives in time to save her. Emily disappears, and later turns up in a new facility, where Lionel tells Dinsmore that the clone is LuthorCorp property, and Dinsmore is off the project.

Lionel offers Lex a two-week private island honeymoon, but Lex refuses. He also takes back control of the Kawatche caves.

LIONEL: I knew you had your vices, son, but I didn't realize gluttony was one of them.

LEX: Well, I suppose if there's anyone who's an authority on the seven deadly sins, it's you, Dad.

"I love 'Accelerate' — it's one of my top five *Smallville* episodes," Ken Biller maintains. "Any time you have little kids gone bad, it's creepy. It was an opportunity to tell a ghost story, only we had a really different *Smallville* explanation for it. 'Accelerate' is well-written, well-acted, and well-directed by James Marshall."

"The little girl was amazing," John Glover recalls. "She was sick the day we filmed the final scene together, but she was terrific. I remember James Marshall took the scene and showed it to Al, and said we should keep that last bit, because I think the editors were ready to snip it out." "John Glover embraced that scene," David Willson recalls.

Opposite: Lana discovers the clone of Emily.

SMALLVILLE MUSIC

'I'm With You' by Avril Lavigne

"Lionel took devilish pleasure in torturing that little girl!"

"You never know where you'll find a kid," Greg Beeman points out. "Or even *if* you'll find one. I've done a lot of children's movies, but this little girl walked in, and she was so haunting and frightening, and at the same time empathetic. Imagine if we hadn't found her and had some cutified little Barbie-doll actress!"

LANA: If I could go back and change that day, I swear to you I would. I live every day knowing that it should have been me.
EMILY: This time it will be.

"'Accelerate' came out of a conversation about what Lionel was doing with the kryptonite that he had in the vault," Al Gough says. "The idea of cloning people using kryptonite as an accelerator was fascinating. I loved the ending with Lionel and the girl and the bunny — you understand that the Level 3 experiments have continued."

"The biggest problem we had with the whole episode was that the location they chose for the river turned into an actual raging torrent on the day we went to shoot," Mike Walls recalls. "It was so slippery up there, it was unbelievable."

"We were on a bridge in Capilano, and they had me tethered up, and then Emily would push me and I'd pretend to fall, and hang over the end," Kristin Kreuk explains. "There was no actual fall — they shoved a rock down. The river was so high that they couldn't do it. Then they cut to a tiny little tank, where I sank down and pretended to be dead, then Tom and I did the rescue scene down there. It was the first time I'd spent all day in the water!"

Below: Lana relives her youth with her childhood friend.

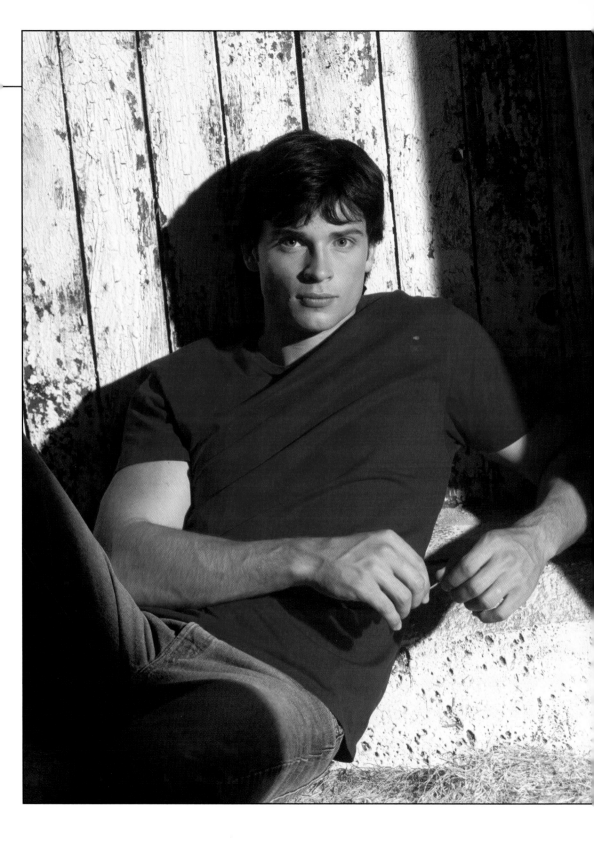

Smallville 🐓 Ledger

★ ★ ★ Volume 65, Number 11 ★ ★ ★

BRYCE/LUTHOR ENGAGEMENT

Smallville residents Dr. Helen Bryce and Lex Luthor have announced their engagement. The couple plan to wed in May of this year.

Metropolis natives Bryce and Luthor met in Smallville several months ago and instantly fell in love.

The bride and groom have hired Metropolis wedding planner Zoe Flite to organize the big event. Flite stated, "Normally I like to have at least twelve months in order to plan this type of spectacular wedding. It's going to be a challenge to arrange this in only a few weeks. And Lex has insisted that I use only local vendors in order to 'keep the money in the community'. At first I didn't know anyone else here — except for the two of them — but I'm learning fast. And everyone has been extremely helpful and friendly. Helen and Lex's wedding will be fantastic. I promise."

Lana Lang, Talon manager and Luthor's business partner, reported, "I've never seen Lex so happy. He's met his match in Helen. I definitely approve."

By Kathy Romita

The stunning sequence in the cemetery where Clark and Emily superspeed through the rain was a scene that "Miles and Al had been pushing for for some time," Greg Beeman recalls. "We'd never had the opportunity, or money, to do it."

By not using many visual effects in either 'Precipice' or 'Witness', Entity FX were allowed to spend the time and money on researching and implementing the scene. "The trick was to create something that's not only superspeeding to advance the story, but also has a cool look," Mat Beck explains. "We used the Houdini™ software package to generate the raindrops. Each raindrop can be thought of as a lens, as a mirror, and an object in itself. The entire backdrop is refracted through it like a lens, and the area behind the camera is being reflected in it. By adjusting those parameters, we were able to give it a brilliant jewel-like magical quality. We figured that round drops weren't that interesting, and teardrop ones looked a little silly and over the top, so we settled on this round diamond shape."

As Clark goes through the drops, there are little explosions as he hits them. "We had our 3-D department calculate a bunch of collision events, which went up to 2-D, and we dropped in little splashes whenever he hit a drop," Beck continues. "Eli Jarra also added a mist trail behind him. I was watching all the cars on the freeways throwing up these loose trails of spray in the rainstorms we were having at the time. We took some liberties to make it all look cooler." (Mat Beck isn't the only one to think it looked cool: it's another shot that later won a Visual Effects Society Award.) ∎

DID YOU KNOW?

The mist on the pods containing the clones of Emily was created by Entity FX to make the scene more mysterious.

CALLING

WRITTEN BY: Kenneth Biller
DIRECTED BY: Terrence O'Hara

GUEST STARS: Rob LaBelle (Dr. Frederick Walden),
Emmanuelle Vaugier (Dr. Helen Bryce), Terence Stamp
(Voice of Jor-El)

Dr. Walden wakes from his coma (see 'Rosetta') screaming that 'the day is coming'. He breaks out of the hospital after burning a symbol on the ceiling and returns to the cave. He then triggers a change in the writing on the wall. Clark tells his parents that the new cave symbols mean, 'The day is coming when the last son will begin his quest to rule the third planet.' Walden bursts in on a meeting between the Luthors and, before he is subdued, claims that the symbols say that Clark Kent is going to rule the world. At his wedding rehearsal dinner, Lex tells Clark about Walden's claims, and Clark is later drawn back to the farm, where Walden is waiting to kill him. Walden dies in the ensuing fight, clutching the key in his scorched hand. Clark retrieves the key, but it has left an imprint on Walden's palm. Lionel later has the hand removed from the body by the coroner.

Clark's blood sample is stolen from Helen's office, and Jonathan believes Lex was involved. Helen finds a file on Martha in Lex's office but he denies involvement in the theft — although the vial is really in his possession. Chloe tries to reconcile with Clark, but he is hesitant. Lionel asks her to investigate Clark, and she refuses — but when she walks into his barn, she sees Clark and Lana admitting to their feelings and kissing. Chloe leaves, unnoticed, in tears. That night, Clark hears a voice saying, "Kal-El, it is time," and heads for the storm cellar...

HELEN: Mr. Kent, Lex is not the man you think he is.

JONATHAN: Considering the fact that you are about to spend the rest of your life with that man, and what you know about my family, you had better be right.

"'Calling' is a hard episode," Greg Beeman points out. "It's like 'Vortex'; structurally and artistically it's a very difficult type of episode to write and direct because it doesn't conclude. It's the episode before the finale, so it's all foreplay. There weren't a lot of visual effects or explosions to gild the lily either. But Terrence O'Hara is really our strongest performance director, along with James Marshall, and the episode resonated."

Ken Biller agrees about the structural problems. "The second to last episode always tends to be weaker," he notes. "With this one, there were two very different storylines going on, which felt incongruous in a way. You have all this emotional stuff going on with Clark, and the preparations for the wedding, but every time you cut away to Dr. Walden, you feel like you're in a different movie. But there is some really cool stuff. The

Opposite: Lex wonders what is puzzling Clark.

Above: Together at last – Lana and Clark celebrate his birthday.

Themes from *Superman: The Movie* by John Williams
'In This Life' by Chantal Kreviazuk
'Signs of Love' by Moby
'Wastin' My Time' by Boomkat
'Telling You Now' by Jessy Moss
'Everything to Me' by Elza

notion of this crazy lunatic guy downloaded with information that Clark was downloaded with, walking around ranting and raving that Clark is the Anti-Christ, was really interesting — and then he comes and confronts Lex with this information, right in front of Lionel!"

Rob LaBelle recalls that the episode gave him the opportunity to indulge in "a limited amount of stunt work. It's always a kick doing those kinds of things — it's muddy and raining and you get into the whole thing! The stunt guys on *Smallville*, particularly Christopher Sayour, are incredible, and to watch them working was really a pleasure. There was one shot where I blast Clark out of the barn, and normally a stuntman would just fly back on a pulley. Christopher wanted to make it different, so he did a half twist in the middle in the air, and came down. He wanted to make it look dynamic, so he went that extra mile."

LaBelle was concerned in case Walden appeared too over the top. "Yes, the guy's crazy a little bit," he agrees, "and he's been in the hospital in a catatonic state. He comes out and he's got a heat beam coming out of his hand. But he's not a bad guy. He may come across as evil, but he's not. He's read the hieroglyphs, which say that this guy will come and take over the world. Walden is trying to save the world, save humankind by battling the superhuman alien creature. It's an absurd situation, but as an actor you've got to balance it."

"The trick with the fight between Clark and Walden was choreographing things," Mat Beck recalls. "We put Walden up in the air, and we wanted the energy beam suspending him to bend a little bit as it went through, because that has a certain amount of energy. The heat vision had to cross that, so we had to arrange the frame so that it looked like a good three dimensional image, but you see all of those pieces do their thing."

CHLOE: Mr. Luthor, I don't know what your interest is in Clark, but you can take the job offer and shove it down your thousand dollar pants.

LIONEL: Clark's very lucky to have a friend like you. All that integrity. I wonder, though, if he had to make a choice, would he sacrifice his dream out of loyalty to you?

The episode was originally intended to begin with Clark and Lana watching a comet through Clark's telescope. "Clark had got Lana to stay up very late at night to try and watch this with him," Ken Biller recalls, "and you saw the comet bursting in the background. The comet heralded the arrival of Jor-El, Clark having to leave, and Walden waking up. There was a lot of language and imagery about the comet and something that beautiful being worth the wait, which threw them into the romantic moment. However, the comet was an expensive effect, and there didn't seem to be a reason to mention it if you couldn't see the comet!"

"'Calling' is a lot of the wind-up, but not necessarily the pitch," Al Gough concludes. "As you get toward the end of the season, you know where the cliffhanger is going to be. The shows along the way are fun, because you know you're winding up to some really big things. 'Calling' really laid the foundation for 'Exodus'..." ∎

Smallville 🐓 Ledger

★ ★ ★ Volume 65, Number 12 ★ ★ ★

BREAK-IN AT S.M.C.

Dr. Helen Bryce arrived at the Smallville Medical Center for work to discover her office had been ransacked. Her confidential papers were strewn across the floor, desk drawers dumped and filing cabinets opened. Apparently bolt cutters were used to break into a normally locked refrigerated specimen case — only an empty test tube rack remained inside. Dr. Bryce was overheard telling her fiancé "nothing valuable was stolen".

There were no witnesses and unfortunately no security cameras in this area of the medical center. Police have no suspects at this time. Deputy Sheriff Elizabeth Christine said, "Drugs may be a motive for the burglary, or the vandalism was a cleverly staged ruse to cover up what the thief was really after."

By Angie Perez

EXODUS

WRITTEN BY: Alfred Gough
& Miles Millar
DIRECTED BY: Greg Beeman

GUEST STARS: Emmanuelle Vaugier (Dr. Helen Bryce),
Terence Stamp (Voice of Jor-El)

'Strange & Beautiful (I'll Put
a Spell On You)' by Aqualung
'High On Sunshine' by Kelly Brock
'Take Me Away' by Lifehouse
'Weapon' by Matthew Good
Themes from *Superman: The
Movie* by John Williams
'Jesu Joy of Man's Desiring'
(Bach arr. Snow)

The voice from the ship explains that he is Clark's father, Jor-El, and it is time for Clark to follow his destiny. Clark doesn't want to leave, but is told he has no choice. Lex admits he stole the blood, and Helen calls the wedding off, although she later returns. Lionel has made a kryptonite copy of the key which he tells Clark he intends to use to decipher the symbols. That evening the ship brands Clark with an ancestral mark, and Jor-El tells him that if he doesn't leave by noon, he will hurt those he loves.

The next day, Clark and Pete steal the kryptonite key from Lionel. Jonathan gives Lex a compass as a wedding present, but when Lana turns up alone at the wedding, the Kents leave. Clark puts the kryptonite key into the spaceship, which explodes, sending out a shockwave which causes the Kents' truck to crash.

Lex and Helen leave for their honeymoon on the LuthorCorp jet. Clark goes with his parents to the hospital, where they learn that Martha has lost the baby. Devastated, Clark returns home where he tells Lana that he's a danger to everyone. Chloe agrees to investigate Clark for Lionel, while Lex wakes to find himself alone on the plane, crashing into the sea.

Clark takes one of the red kryptonite rings from Chloe's desk, and despite Lana's pleas to stay, gets on his motorbike and heads for Metropolis… ∎

Smallville Ledger

★ ★ ★ Volume 65, Number 13 ★ ★ ★

LOCAL TEEN RUNS AWAY AFTER MYSTERIOUS BLAST

Smallville High School student Clark Kent has disappeared after an unexplained underground explosion destroyed the family storm cellar, leaving a giant crater in its wake. Jonathan and Martha Kent, who themselves suffered injuries in the explosion, have filed a missing persons report with Sheriff Adams. According to police, Lana Lang was the last person to see the young Kent. "He felt responsible for the accident and his parents getting hurt. He said it was best he leave before anyone else got hurt. But I know Clark, and there's no way he would — could — hurt anyone," said Lana sadly. The Kents would only say, "We love our son. Clark, son, please come home." Police are looking for the teen in the Metropolis area.

The cause of the blast is undetermined, but the eruption did disrupt the power supply to parts of Lowell County.

By Shelby Taylor

Opposite: A few moments of
happiness for Clark and Lana.

EXODUS: IN DEPTH

"To have two very strong father figures telling you different things is a lot to handle, and Clark has to take this information, put it to the test and come to his own conclusion, and it's not an easy one." — Tom Welling

"I liked 'Exodus' very much," Al Gough says. "At the beginning of the episode Clark has everything he ever wanted, and by the end of it, he has nothing. Season one ended with the height of heroism, with Clark running into a tornado to save Lana. For season two, we wanted to see the nadir of that, which is Clark running away. He gets on 'drugs' [the red kryptonite], gets on his motorbike, and runs away from his problems. In the journey to become a super hero, these are the sorts of trials you're going to face. And was it what Jor-El planned all along?"

In addition to exploring the mythology of the series further, 'Exodus' also served a practical purpose. "Quite honestly, we wanted to get rid of the spaceship," Gough points out. "Once the props start talking, you've got to be careful! We wanted to blow it up and be done with it. We had the caves, so we still had a Kryptonian connection, but we'd played the ship. How many times are people going to go to the storm cellar? We wanted to be rid of it, but we wanted to do it in a big way."

The episode also returns to the series' theme of extreme parenting. "It's about an adopted child finding out who his birth parents are and realizing he doesn't like these people, and trying to get away from them," Gough notes. "Clark thinks he can destroy the ship, and realizes that literally and figuratively, he can't keep his problems locked in the storm cellar, and that his actions have consequences and repercussions. Then he leaves — it's like the ending of *The Empire Strikes Back*. He's scarred and runs away, leaving everybody he loves."

Executive producer Greg Beeman, who had also directed the previous season finale, admits that he was more concerned about 'Exodus' than 'Tempest'. "Miles and Al had told me what the beats of the story were a long time before we started," he explains. "I was nervous about it to some degree. I was not nervous about Lana's truck being lifted up and Clark flying into the tornado in 'Tempest' — I knew that was going to work right away. I wasn't as confident about Clark putting on the red kryptonite ring and riding off to Metropolis. I had to pump myself up that I was going to make this work. I wasn't convinced at all that Clark was going to have *so* many terrible tragedies happen to him — that he would go through *such* despair — he was going to be driven to put on the red K ring and leave forever."

Executive producer Ken Horton always likes to have a good idea of what's coming up at the end of the season, so he can plan the post-production elements. "My involvement conceptually came very early," he recalls. "It was probably around January 2003 when we were sitting around discussing the finale, because you really do have to start thinking about it around that time."

Opposite: A pensive Clark Kent.

Horton has worked on many long-running series, and is aware of the importance of the end of season cliffhanger. "They are very interesting," he says. "If you do them wrong, you just annoy the audience. If you do the cliffhanger right, but the resolve doesn't have enough juice, the audience gets annoyed retroactively — 'We waited four months for *this*?' So you have to be very careful. The audience is now accustomed to big stories, big events and big emotional arcs." "You always want to end big," visual effects producer Mat Beck agrees. "We didn't need warning that this was going to be huge. We saved up our nickels for the big event and, in production terms, made sure we had our resources in place."

As far as the on-set work was concerned, executive producer Bob Hargrove points out that 'Exodus' contained "nothing outside the norm for *Smallville*. It was just a big episode. There were a lot of elements involved in that show that just made it bigger, from exploding holes to sound waves — and a few things that didn't end up in the finished product. We can always count on our last show of the season being bigger than others, so we are prepared for that."

The cooperation between departments that ensures *Smallville* runs so smoothly is of paramount importance. "Miles and Al know these shows are ambitious," Hargrove continues. "They tend to give us a good head start of what's coming. These are not shows you can prep in eight days. 'Exodus' was a very visual effects-intensive show, so we had a lot of things to prepare in terms of greenscreens and back plates, and digging the hole at the Kent farm."

The opening scene of 'Exodus' follows directly on from 'Calling', as Clark follows the mysterious voice down into the storm cellar, and sees the spaceship glowing. "We got Terence Stamp to play Jor-El," Al Gough notes, "because we wanted someone from the Superman mythos, and he was happy to do it." Stamp's role as the villainous General Zod in the first two Christopher Reeve movies made some fans wonder whether this wasn't Jor-El at all, but Zod in disguise. It's a fun theory, but when asked at ComicCon two months after the episode aired, Gough stated bluntly that this wasn't the case.

The scene, like many, was an effects-heavy sequence. "From a story standpoint, it seems that Clark has not been sent to be a good guy on Earth, but an emperor," Mat Beck points out. "He has to deal with that moral conflict, and that idea was reflected in the effects. Along with his gifts, he has an enormous amount of pain and burden. The ship was completely computer generated for this sequence, since it went through so many permutations. The sequence was very elaborately scripted out, so that the ship turns into a glowing orb with this robotic clankety-clank, which was described as 'like a work of futuristic origami'. Well, the concept of origami works on paper!

"Then the ship changes into the Earth," Beck continues, "which then has an eclipse go across it to have a glowing corona. The light changes at the same moment as it changes into the Earth, which was a cool moment, and it was also eloquent to see the Earth. It's like your mother's face — it's an evocative image." Beck admits he was a little

Above: Clark prepares to face his destiny.

concerned about the shot. "Planetary bodies floating in a storm cellar can be a problem, but it came together pretty well."

Clark then turns to see images of his parents and Lana. "It's a touching moment when they look at each other," Beck notes, "but it was a struggle to make that particular effect look fresh."

CLARK: Everything and everyone I love is here! In Smallville!
JOR-EL: You must let go of your past. I will guide you to your future.
CLARK: No, I don't want your guidance! I want to create my own future!
JOR-EL: You have no choice, Kal-El.

When Clark tells his parents what's happened, the incidental music features some of John Williams' score from the Krypton sequence in *Superman: The Movie*. The music had made its first appearance in 'Rosetta'. "We put the John Williams music in as a temp track on the cut of 'Rosetta' that went to the studio," Ken Horton recalls, "and they called back and said we had to use it. I assumed it would cost us a squidillion dollars to do, but Mr. Williams said okay somewhere along the line, and we gave it to Mark Snow.

Above: Lex prepares to face
his destiny.

We couldn't use the original because we would have to pay the orchestra, so Mark went back and did a version."

When it came to film the next scene, in which Helen walks out on Lex, Emmanuelle Vaugier was beginning to wonder whether Dr. Bryce was as genuine as she seemed. "I had an idea that maybe I was being pushed over to the dark side," she admits, "and I was thinking, 'Damn, if only I could have stayed good a little longer…'"

Michael Rosenbaum admits that he *did* know whether Helen was on his side or not by the time he came to film 'Exodus', but "I didn't tell Emmanuelle. She asked me, but I said, 'No.' She had no idea!"

Emmanuelle Vaugier is glad that she didn't know for certain. "In order for it to be believable, you have to play it that she doesn't have ulterior motives," she says. "There's nothing going on. It's all in Lex's mind, and she's just trying to make things work. The audience has to believe she's really honest and good, because they're just waiting for any of Lex's love interests to turn evil and try to kill him."

Rosenbaum was delighted that Greg Beeman was in charge of this episode. "Boy, do I love that guy," he enthuses. "You can't make this show without Greg Beeman. What keeps a show successful are people who are passionate about the job, and he's one of those guys."

Beeman himself points out that "I have to get into an emotional place to channel the emotions of an episode. Then I try to visualize the style, and replicate that emotional feel. On 'Exodus', I knew it had to be sad and have a despair to it. It was very difficult and arduous for me emotionally. I was going through a negotiation with Warner Bros. where I was being asked to come back to *Smallville*, and at that moment in time, it wasn't going very well. That ultimately served the picture well, because I had a certain amount of despair through that whole episode personally, because I really didn't know if I was going to be coming back or not. I thought this might be my last episode ever, and in some ways that was the same emotion that Clark was having. That agitated upsetness was the emotion of that show, and I don't know whether I channeled it in some 'Method'-y way, or I made a decision to use it, but I knew that Clark had to be in despair, and that was a color that Tom had never played on the show."

Clark and his father watch what may be his final sunset in Smallville. Mat Beck knew that the "shot was a very tight balance. It's a glowing, spectacular sunset, and when you put people in front of that in the real world they sometimes look phony, because the lighting is so outrageous. We had to strive for a balance, in which it looked like they were conceivably there."

Clark returns to the cellar "and stands up to the voice of his father," Beck continues, "and for his trouble gets knocked up into the upper corner of the cellar and gets a high-temperature tattoo job on his chest."

"Brian Harding did a lot of really nice work on the tattoo," Mat Beck notes. "The idea was to make it look like it's burning out of his chest from the inside. Any effect integrated with human skin is always challenging, because tracking it from one shot to another is always an adventure."

The effects team also had to perform one of their 'invisible' effects — something you wouldn't realize was an effect unless told. "You see Clark's chest get burned, and then in a wide shot, you see him drop to the ground," Beck explains. "The stunt guy had a T-shirt on, hiding the harness he was wearing, and so we had to paint the chest in digitally as he drops, before cutting into a reverse shot of a bare-chested Tom dropping to the ground."

The second act begins with the first scene shot at the Kent farm, as Clark sees his parents off to Lex's wedding. "That day was insane," physical effects supervisor Mike Walls recalls. "It was system overload for me, for Greg, for the director of photography

Below: Brian Harding's original design for Clark's Kryptonian tattoo.

Barry Donlevy — for a whole pile of people. We had four units shooting simultaneously: a helicopter unit, an insert car unit, the main unit with the actors, and a splinter unit trying to get ready on everything, and do stunts at the same time. We had to run from one spot to the next to the next, getting things done."

Greg Beeman had some very specific ideas in mind when he shot the scene between Clark and Lana in the barn — which, although it looks like it's part of the location filming, is actually on the stages in Burnaby. "Usually when I direct I have a song in mind," he explains. "I fought to get the Coldplay song for the end of 'Vortex'. For 'Exodus', I heard this song 'Weapon' by Matthew Good, who's big in Canada, but not very well known in the rest of the world. The lyrics talk about an angel by my side, and the Devil by my side, and I directed this scene to that song. I had timed out in my mind what shots were going to go with what lyrics to what move. I told Tom and Kristin that we were using this song, and they're used to 'Beeman having a song', but I didn't tell them how specific it was. It's a luxury, and very rare in any medium to have a scene that's really important, with a lot of emotional moments but almost no dialog. I love that kind of thing. I'm an acting-based director, so I'm happy to let the acting play, not the words."

CHLOE: Newsflash. You've always been in love with Lana. I tried to deny it, thinking that maybe we could work something out, but it's like fate, Clark. Inevitable, but always surprising when it actually happens.

Beeman worked very closely with Tom Welling to get the emotions he wanted. After Chloe has abandoned him to "have a nice life", and not knowing that his parents are

Right: Clark tries and fails to explain himself to Chloe.

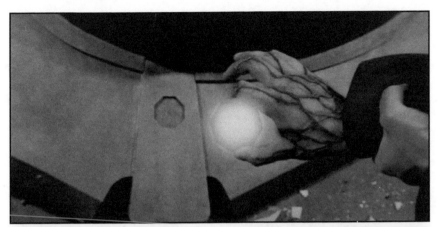

Left: Clark inserts the fake key into
the ship, triggering devastation.

racing back to the farm, Clark descends to the storm cellar to destroy the ship with the kryptonite key. "Tom and I worked a lot on that very visceral scene," Beeman recalls.

"It's a big enough decision to destroy the ship, but Clark doesn't just have to decide, he has to pick up a piece of kryptonite and plug it in," Mat Beck says. "It instantly starts messing with him. We had some practical marks on Tom's skin that we could track to, and then put some digital veins on top which were tracked to those marks, and revealed themselves as he was holding the key.

"Then he drops the key into the ship," Beck continues, "and we were going for some sort of virus/fungus growing out, some sort of fractal decay. The challenge was to make it look interesting, dynamic and not too pretty. It was green tinged with gold, and we had to desaturate the color and rust it up a little bit. Mike McCormick did a nice job having it grow like a really nasty skin infection, and as it grew outward, it revealed a certain amount of structure inside the skin, as if roots were growing, or it was following some sort of circulatory system. Then we had to show distress in this mechanical device. It got some tremors, which were a balance, because if they were too extreme, it would definitely look like an effect. But it got the idea across that this was one sick ship."

The nature of the ship's demise was the subject of major discussion. "Originally it was going to be a huge explosion," Beck says, "but the problem was that nobody wanted to destroy the farm and build it up again. So it was determined that it was more like an electromagnetic pulse [EMP]."

"We did a shot of the farm set from a helicopter, pulling back from the point of impact," visual effects supervisor John Wash adds. "We were going to have some sparks traveling along the power lines," Beck recalls, "but that shot got dropped. There was a lot of tweaking to figure out what explodes, and what do we see after the explosion?"

As Wash points out, "How do you bring concreteness to a script that says 'a massive shockwave fans out like a tsunami'? We had to start with a lot of ideas and see if something clicked. The animators started with one idea, but we had to say it wasn't working and make a 180-degree shift from what we were going for. It was one of the very last shots we delivered."

"We had some practical explosion shots, and an aerial shot where we could see the crater from the very beginning," Mat Beck amplifies. "We had to hide the crater digitally so we could reveal it later. We decided that the ship would extend a column of light into the air, and that would collapse down into a ripple that spread across the land. That would create the crater, and have a rhythm to it. There was an implosion before the explosion, so we tried to make it look like the soil was sinking down, and then when we were cutting it together, it became apparent we needed a moment between the implosion and the explosion." The only way this could be achieved was by shortening another part of the sequence to allow a moment of stillness. "We stole some frames to give us that beat," Beck reveals.

The column of light collapses into a torus of energy that radiates across the landscape away from the Kent farm, sending Martha and Jonathan off the road. "The gag with the

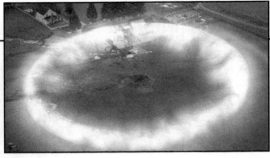

Above: The EMP pulse radiates from the Kent farm.

truck was a cool idea that stuntman Tony Morelli came up with," Christopher Sayour recalls. "We had the truck with the stuntman and stuntwoman come sliding in, then we dropped the telephone pole, and Mike Walls hit some sparks, and as it landed, we had the stunt player slide into the pole. Then we put some dummies in the truck, wrapped it in a cable, and propelled it off a ratchet to make it roll."

"The first time, the telephone pole didn't come down," Mike Walls adds. "Everything blew apart the way it was supposed to, but there was about half an inch of wood holding everything up, which was very disheartening!" Once the stunt had been successfully pulled off, it was time to shoot close-ups of Jonathan and Martha in the flipped over truck. "We built an incredible sliding rig to get John and Annette into the truck," Walls reveals. "Putting them in a truck upside down is rather tricky, and we didn't want them in there for any length of time. So we built the seat on a rig, so we could bring it out and spin it. They sat in it right side up, and we strapped them in, spun them upside down on the pole, and pushed them into the truck. That worked really well!"

In the final version of the scene, the EMP itself sends Jonathan off the road. "We constructed that sequence out of the pieces we had," Mat Beck explains. "We made it plausible that the energy wave makes him go off the road. We had the wide shot of the donut expanding outward from the farm, then the Kents' point-of-view of this great big wall of shimmering nastiness coming toward them. We cut to a shot of Annette, with the EMP playing on the windshield, and then to a wide shot of the truck coming through the intersection. For that we had to move stuff all over the place, reconstituting the frame to put the truck where it would be so it was in the right space for the subsequent collision, and then we cut to the rolling truck, for which we had to do the wire removals."

In the aftermath of the explosion, we see Clark in the remnants of the storm cellar. "The art department did a great job on that," Greg Beeman notes, and wryly recalls making the star of the show even dirtier than he already was. "Everyone laughs at me, because whenever it's time for the actors to be dirty or bloody, inevitably I think they come out of make-up looking twenty percent of what they need to be. So Tom Welling comes out, and I say, 'Hand me the bag of dirt!' and Welling sighs, 'Here we go,' as I'm smearing dirt on him…"

Beeman worked very hard with Tom and John Schneider on the scenes in the hospital where Clark admits what he's done. "There are some scenes in that where you're looking at two backs," he comments. "Sometimes you have to fight against the

EXODUS: IN DEPTH

regimented rules which say that if emotions are happening, or people are talking, you have to see their faces. I shot that scene as lots of two-shots, seeing both actors at the same time. There's one moment where we're on Clark's back and you know exactly what he's thinking — ironically his back is more powerful than his face because of the shame he feels."

It was appropriate that the destruction of the ship was responsible for Martha's miscarriage since "the ship had allowed Martha to conceive," Al Gough explains. "At the end of the season, we knew that Jor-El was going to come and say that it was time for Clark to leave, and in a weird way, it was giving the Kents something for when he was going to take Clark away. It's somewhat insidious — 'These people did their job, so I'll give them the ability to have a child. Now I'm going to take my son and train him for his destiny.'"

"The scene with Clark and Lana was very unusual," Greg Beeman recalls. "I took Tom aside and told him about the place of despair that he had to get to. I talked to him like a coach, and then staged the scene and rolled camera. And he did it. It was awesome! I knew he was never going to perform it this good again. You thought he really was shell-shocked and dazed. I did one take, and said, 'Cut! Print!' checked there were no technical problems, and went to move on. Tom was amazed, but I told him he would never do it that good again. He channeled the emotion I wanted."

As Chloe decides, in Allison Mack's words, to "flirt with the dark side", Clark raids her school drawers looking for one of the red kryptonite class rings. "That's the place where we pay off red K," co-executive producer Ken Biller explains. "Now we really see him go 'on drugs' to salve his own pain and his guilt about what he's done. We successfully set up a bunch of different cliffhangers here, and it really just rocks and rolls."

"I worked very hard on the emotional build with Tom's character," Greg Beeman adds.

"I was really nervous about that last scene where Kristin was crying and saying, 'I love you.' But it went well."

One of Mat Beck's favorite moments is when Clark slips the red K ring onto his finger. "We watch the veins move up his arm, with the glowy red vein effect, which is like a green vein effect except for the wavelength of the light, and then it goes up to his eyes. Tom did this move, almost like Homer Simpson with a turkey leg, and we added a little red flicker in his eyes. It's a great example of the interaction between good acting and visual effects. It's an important moment — our main character is making a decision, and it's not one his drug counselor would agree with."

LANA: The Clark Kent I know wouldn't run away from his problems.
CLARK: The Clark Kent you know is a lie.

Lex, meanwhile, is discovering he's in serious trouble. "Of all the movie-writing talents that Miles and Al have, it's when they write the cliffhangers that you can really see it," Ken Horton says. "They clearly understand how to set an audience up!"

The scenes on the LuthorCorp jet were shot on a gimbaled set to allow the necessary movement, and directed by first assistant director Bryan Knight. "James Marshall wasn't able to finish 'Accelerate'," Greg Beeman explains, "because weather had caused us to delay second unit stuff with Kristin and the little girl on the bridge. I felt it was more important for the good of the series that I go direct that emotional stuff, and I gave Bryan Knight the tap to go over the boards, to use a hockey metaphor, and direct the scenes in the plane."

"How far did we want to take that crashing cockpit?" Mat Beck queries. "Ken said, 'Hell — make the water come right through the cockpit!' We added some more cables to give some more chaos, and shook the hell out of everything. In the very last frames, we made it look as if the water was coming through the cockpit. It was our homage to Cast Away — done in three days on a considerably constricted budget!"

The final scene sees Clark disappearing off on his bike, "off out of the plains of Kansas toward Metropolis," Mat Beck comments. "Before we could add Metropolis in the distance, we had to do a certain amount of evergreen forest and mountain removal! Brian added a few fake hills in there, and the road went round a couple of fake turns before heading for Metropolis."

The episode ends with Mark Snow's score combining his own music with John Williams' Krypton theme, as well as the Superman fanfare. "It seems to take the show into another dimension," Snow comments. "It's amazing, the simplicity of those melodies — and yet the effect is staggering."

Al Gough is pleased with the end result. "We set up that Jor-El might have a more malevolent agenda for Clark," he notes. "Superman doesn't live in the dark, that's not his world, but you have to understand that in his journey he's going to be faced with these things, and sometimes he's going to screw up and fail. If you don't do that, I don't think you've done the character justice." ∎

CLARK KENT

"I've got all these questions, and I can't leave them in the storm cellar any more. Why did my parents put me in that ship? What was so bad they had to send me away?"

During the second season of *Smallville*, Clark Kent begins to learn far more about his Kryptonian heritage, courtesy of the mysterious Dr. Virgil Swann. He also experiences the effects of other forms of kryptonite for the first time. For Tom Welling, both of these new facets to his character gave him an opportunity to expand his range on the show.

He thoroughly enjoys the chance to put on his class ring and play the red kryptonite-infected Clark. "It's so much fun," he grins. "It's like the bird getting out of the cage, both for me and for the character. I hope we see more of him — he's fun to play, and entertaining for the audience to watch. I think it also shakes things up for the other characters."

Certainly, Clark loses many of his inhibitions when the red kryptonite affects his brain. "He gets the chance to get a lot of things off his chest, which either he felt he wasn't able to bring up, or knew that it wasn't a good thing to bring up, especially with his parents and Lana," Tom explains. It doesn't mean that Clark's no longer aware of the consequences of what he's saying and doing, however. "He just doesn't care," Tom continues. "He simply doesn't care. People have referred to him as 'Dark Clark' or 'Bad Clark', but I think of him as a Clark with no inhibitions. When Clark goes to Metropolis at the end of 'Exodus', not only do people die, but they die or get hurt because of him. I like the fact that we're showing the consequences of his actions more and more."

Tom is delighted to note that unlike on some shows, the producers don't press a 'reset button' at the end of the red kryptonite episodes, so that at the start of the following episode everyone, including Clark, has forgotten what he said and did while he was affected. "That doesn't happen on our show," Tom says. "Clark is normally very aware of the consequences of his actions — maybe too much sometimes. With 'Red Clark' he's *completely* aware of the consequences of his actions at the time, but he doesn't care! He doesn't care what happens to you, and he certainly doesn't care what happens to himself, because he probably realizes that nothing can happen to him. It's always fun to be that way, even in real life, because we're not allowed to be that way all too often."

Tom has fond memories of working with Christopher Reeve on 'Rosetta'. "He is probably the most knowledgeable guy on Superman in the world!" he laughs. "I also think he's the definition of a hero — someone who does things for purposes beyond their own desires and wants in life. He's quite an inspiration: he's a man who was remarkable even before the incident [that crippled him] and has just used it to make the most of the situation. Even his foundation, which is doing so well, has never been about him, it's been about the cause. He's a great guy and we both had a really good time doing it."

Reeve's knowledge of Superman contrasted greatly with Tom, who has always been happy to learn about Clark Kent's life from what he is given in the scripts from episode to episode. After their scenes were shot in the *Third Watch* offices in New York, Clark Kents past and present gave a press conference together, and Tom was on the receiving end of some of Christopher Reeve's humor. "We were being interviewed, and they were asking Christopher about Superman and what he would do," Tom recalls, "and Christopher was saying, 'Shush — he's not supposed to hear this yet! He doesn't know who this Superman is! Don't tell him.' And it's true — they're two very different characters. A lot of the information Christopher had was about a character I don't know, and the character I play differs slightly from the background that he had when he was playing Superman. Our series is much more contemporary than his film was for its day. Except for the name, the two men don't have that much in common."

Tom understands the practical reasons why Clark and Lana are kept apart during the second year. "There's the cliché that television shows with a main love interest fail once they get it together," he notes. "They've got to keep us apart — but you never know what might happen. They've done a great job of bringing us close. The first season I was going after her, and in the second season we got together, then she was going after me.

At the end, in 'Exodus', I have to say to her, 'It's dangerous to be with me.'"

However, Tom does think that Lana might be receptive to hearing the truth from Clark. "It's one of the things we've always talked about behind the camera," he points out. "Clark is always hiding his secret from Lana when in actuality she is probably the one person in the world who would accept him for who he is and be completely understanding."

Clark does, of course, share his secret in season two with his oldest friend, Pete Ross, and Tom was delighted with this shift in the dynamic. "Pete brings a fun side to it, where he can get Clark to try to have fun with these powers of his," he laughs. "He wants to know how far Clark can throw something. He's in a different environment with Pete, who wants to have fun, than he is with Jonathan. His father is always telling Clark to keep his powers suppressed, and only use them at certain times. Maybe that's one thing that Clark will learn before he becomes Superman — how to be in control of himself in any environment, rather than floating between how he feels around Pete, and then around Lana."

Tom relishes the energy that flows in the scenes between Jonathan, Clark and Lex. "Those scenes are so interesting," he says, "because although Lex isn't bad yet, it's like the

red devil and the white angel on Clark's shoulders. Both Lex and Jonathan have very good reasons why they think Clark should act in a particular fashion, and they're always fun scenes to do. In the first season, everything was very black and white with Jonathan, but now he's bending a little bit. Some of the things he's agreed to let Clark do this year, he wouldn't have earlier."

It's a tough life playing Clark Kent, and Tom is on set virtually every day, in the majority of scenes. "But I've had the opportunity to have what they call 'on the job' training," he explains, "and I've learned so much about the job itself and the responsibilities I have. It's been a really good learning experience. You get a good environment when everybody feels that they're needed and they're all helping out." ∎

LANA LANG

"I have doubted you, accused you of things, and still you're here protecting me. I don't care if you have secrets, Clark. You are the one good, constant thing in my life, and I don't want to lose you too."

Kristin Kreuk feels that the second season of *Smallville* continues the evolution of Lana Lang's character, as she starts to move on from being the 'girl next door' and begins to develop into a self-reliant young woman. During the year, Lana, in partnership with Lex Luthor, takes on the ownership of the Talon coffee bar. She also starts to discover some truths about her lineage. Her relationship with Chloe is put to the test when she moves into the Sullivans' home, while her feelings for Clark become more intense as the year draws to its close.

At the start of the year, however, Lana has to come to terms with her feelings for Whitney Fordman, who left Smallville to join the Marines in the season one finale, 'Tempest'. Even before his departure, her attraction to Clark was clearly building, and her growing independence is demonstrated by her decision not to wait for Whitney.

"It's such a hard situation for her to be in," Kristin acknowledges. "She should have told him how she felt about him before he left, but she wasn't strong enough. She decides in the end that she can't lie to him any more: how can she keep telling him that she loves him? It's so the wrong time and the wrong place to say it in the video message, but any other time in the past year would have been the wrong time and the wrong place to do it as well. At the end of 'Red', when she starts to talk to Whitney, I guess she basically went on to say that she's not in love with him. She'll always love him as a friend, and he'll always be a special person to her, but they can't be a couple anymore. Then later on, she tells Chloe that she and Whitney are better friends than they ever were before; they talk to each other more than they had, and they're more open with each other. Whitney loved Lana so much, and he never wanted to hurt her."

The actress thinks that it was a bit of a stretch for the audience to accept that a sixteen-year-old would become part-owner and manager of a coffee shop, but it definitely helped to establish Lana within the series. "It has given her more independence," she confirms. "After Whitney joins the Marines and her aunt leaves, she's got the Talon to ground her. I think it gives her some purpose — it's not like she's just off doing nothing."

The move in with Chloe and her father that takes place when Lana's aunt Nell moves to Metropolis came as something of a surprise to Kristin. She recalls that at one point there was a possibility that Lana might move into the Luthor mansion at this stage, given the relationship between the Langs and the Luthors that had been established during the first season. But Lana and Chloe under the same roof seemed to make for a far more satisfying plotline. "They are both in love with the same person — Clark — and they are very different girls," Kristin explains. "It was very hard for them to really

connect. I think that Lana admires Chloe so much, but I don't think Chloe has as much admiration for Lana. I think Lana sees in Chloe a lot of the traits that she wants to have as a person — the strength, and the ability to say what she wants to say."

It's on Chloe's advice that Lana uses "the hi-tech research device called the doorbell" to find out more about her natural father directly from the horse's mouth — Henry Small. Kristin was very pleased with that plotline, since it continued Lana's discovery of the truth that her parents were not necessarily as perfect as she had imagined, which began in the first year when she found her mother's graduation speech. "Patrick Cassidy was so much fun to work with," Kristin recalls, "and we had really good chemistry together. I think Lana's growth process through the entire show is to become independent, becoming a woman on her own, and meeting her biological father helped her realize that she had this life in her head that didn't really exist. She had to create a new life and be true to herself."

This development in the character means that Lana is beginning to outgrow the innocence that she symbolized at the start of the series. "Every character has the colors they wear which represent something," Kristin points out. "The pink is for innocence and *naïveté*, which I don't think she has anymore. She's losing that — how could she not, with everything going on around her?"

Kristin admits that she was a little taken aback at how quickly Clark and Lana came together as a couple at the end of season two. "It did feel a bit rushed," she says. "It was unexpected for me. After 'Rush', she was pretty upset, then there were just all these little moments between her and Clark through all the episodes leading up to 'Calling'."

The actress considers that it was Lana's encounter with the vengeful clone of her childhood friend Emily Dinsmore that finally pushes Lana into Clark's arms. "I think the events of 'Accelerate' were the button for her," she explains. "That made her wonder why she's holding back, if Clark is so amazing. Should she choose to overlook the fact that she doesn't know a part of who he is? I think she started to understand that Clark really did love her, even though he couldn't share everything with her. So she decides to get involved with him, and I guess it didn't blow up in her face." However, their happiness is destined to be short-lived, as Clark decides at the end of 'Exodus' to leave Smallville and seek his destiny in Metropolis, a decision which leaves Lana shocked and in tears...

Kristin enjoys the physical aspects of the role now, after some initial hesitation. "I did karate for a long time when I was younger," she reveals, "then I did gymnastics until I was in 11th grade, so with all that training, I haven't had to learn very much at all to do the stunts. Right before episodes, I used to maybe do a little bit of training just to make it look a bit better, but now I don't anymore because I'm pretty decent at it. It's all about camera angles and selling it, which is down to the stunt guys. I like doing certain things, and some of it's a lot of fun!" ■

LEX LUTHOR

"You know that darkness you were talking about? I'm not sure we're born with it. I think people like my father find a way to bring it out."

The second season of *Smallville* allows Michael Rosenbaum the freedom to show some of the less pleasant sides of Lex Luthor's personality, from his hesitation over whether to allow his father to die at the start of 'Vortex' and his subsequent shooting of his lackey Roger Nixon at the end of that story, to his angry explosion at Jonathan Kent over the unfair treatment he feels he's received. All of these scenes play to what Michael considers are the series' strengths.

"I think the episodes where you build the bad with the good, and they're character-driven, are the ones that work best," he says. "When you've got Clark and Lana, and Clark and his family, then Lionel heavy with Lex — that contrast mixed together in episodes like 'Insurgence' leads to something phenomenal. The characters are the most important thing about *Smallville*. If you don't like a character, or you don't understand or sympathize with them, then you won't watch a show. People tune in and out really quickly nowadays — and our audience is very smart. I've seen the message boards, and the fans know the show better than any of us!"

Michael notes that for a moment, in the library at the end of 'Tempest' in season one, Lex forgot who he was and nearly allowed his father to die. The ramifications of that moment live with him. "In 'Vortex', you see that Lex felt really guilty about what he'd done," he explains. "He was scared that he'd felt that way. He felt really bad, and realized that he didn't want to go down that path. If he had let Lionel die, then in one way, Lionel would have won — Lex would have become evil, and become everything that Lionel wanted him to be."

However, he's more ambiguous about whether Lex's shooting of Nixon at the end of that episode was the young tycoon's first direct kill. "If it was his first kill, then the audience saw it, and we didn't know if he liked it or not," he says. "But maybe he had killed when he was younger. Who knows? I'm not going to give the answer to that. Maybe it was the first time in a long time that he'd had to do this again, and he didn't want to do it again — he'd tried to stay away from killing, but he ended up doing it again anyway, and it felt good. Maybe it felt right to him — and maybe that scared him..."

The actor is more certain about the causes of Lex's anger toward Jonathan Kent in 'Insurgence'. "Look at Lex's life," he points out. "I would have gone berserk by now if I was living it. I would have said, 'Screw you, Smallville! Go to hell!' But somehow this guy doesn't do that. He's curious, he's brilliant, and he means well — I don't think he always has ulterior motives unless he needs to."

Jonathan Kent's constant needling at him finally breaks Lex's self-control. "I'd been begging the writers for those lines!" Michael admits. "Lex takes a remarkable amount of crap from Jonathan Kent. Somehow he absorbs it, and I think he remembers it,

but because of his love, admiration, and respect for Clark, I think he lets it go. He hears enough of it from his father and the rest of the town that when he hears it from Jonathan Kent, it does infuriate him. But I think he lets it go a little *too* much. The scene where he says that to Jonathan was definitely cathartic: 'Screw you, once and for all!'"

Even then, Lex doesn't explode in uncontrolled rage. "The director wanted me to be more forceful," Michael recalls. "I said, 'No, that's not Lex. It's got to be simple: "I'm tired of this. Go to hell. Enough said."' It was a perfect moment, a well-deserved moment, a needed moment, for the show, for Lex, and for me as an actor."

Michael also enjoyed the scene a little later in the same episode, when Jonathan Kent has to come to beg a ride to Metropolis. "Wasn't that great!" he laughs. "Mr. Kent comes in, and I go, 'I'll give you a ride, Mr. Kent.' That was a really great moment! I wanted the director to know that it was important for me, or rather for my character, to let Mr. Kent squirm for a bit. He wanted me to cut him off straightaway and agree to take him, but I said, 'No, you've got to let him squirm' — and they did. They added to that especially in the editing. There's a beat where the audience is going, 'Come on Lex, say something,' and then finally he lets go and says, 'Yeah, I'll give you a ride to Metropolis.' That's a back-and-forth thing that we do between the writing and the playing. Sometimes the writing is so great that we just say the lines and we don't have to add anything. Sometimes it's the other way around. It's a give and take relationship — when they have little, we make it as big as we can and they're very grateful, and we do the same thing. When we just have to say the lines, it's very easy for us."

With regard to the physical sides of the role, Michael adds, "I try to do as much as I can, but the more the show goes on, the less I do. I had back surgery because I've been playing ice hockey my whole life, so as long it's something that I know I can do without hurting myself, I'll do it. When things feel fun and safe, I definitely want to get involved."

With both Lex and Lionel interested in Clark during the second year, the rift between the farm boy and the young tycoon is slowly drawing nearer. "Ultimately the friendship between Lex and Clark goes away," Michael agrees. "Something happens that's got to be devastating. It's what everybody is waiting for, but it is a journey. You don't want to just give the audience everything. Just when you think Lex is going to get the story, we go off on another path. But all these paths will connect somewhere along the line. The show is about Clark and Lex and Lana — all these relationships. *Smallville* was about characters before it was about the town of Smallville — the writers didn't write about the town first, and then the characters who live there. These are the characters who happen to live in this town, and I think that difference is very important."

Michael considers the success of the show is "everything about it. The way it's shot, the writing, and the characters. If you take any of those away, it wouldn't be the same show. You have to have little elements of each, but ultimately — the characters are the most important part of the show." ■

PETE ROSS

"You think because you have all those powers, you always get your way! News flash! I know your weakness."

Pete Ross's discovery of the Kryptonian spaceship in the cornfield at the start of 'Duplicity' irrevocably altered the friendship that he had shared with Clark Kent since they were young boys. Up until that moment, as with Clark's other friends, Pete hadn't always been able to understand everything that Clark was doing. But once Pete learned that his friend wasn't from Kansas at all, but from another planet altogether, a lot finally started to make sense.

Actor Sam Jones III was delighted when Pete was let in on the secret. "After the first season, the fans were writing into the show, and also commenting on the internet that they wanted to see more Pete," he recalls. "So the writers brought me in and told me that they were thinking about allowing me to know 'the secret'."

Sam believes that Pete's reaction to the news was totally credible. "'Duplicity' was a good episode because most kids, if they were told that someone had these superpowers, would say, 'Really? This is going to be so cool!'" he explains, and while that eventually becomes Pete's attitude toward Clark's abilities, initially he is a lot less happy. "I think it showed a different side to Pete when he just said that he couldn't believe Clark hadn't told him already. He got mad because they were supposed to be friends, and Clark had kept this huge secret. The scene between them in the storm cellar was so powerful because we were watching all the thoughts going through Pete's head. Man, that sort of news would be mind-blowing for anybody!"

Pete's knowledge of the Kents' greatest secret means that not only does Clark have someone other than his parents that he can talk to, but Pete becomes even more involved with the family on a day-to-day basis. He is able to help them when Clark falls under the grip of red kryptonite in 'Red'. For Sam, the episode also demonstrates the strength of the friendship between the two buddies. "During the whole of that story, Pete's trying to be a friend to Clark," he says. "At the beginning, they're just two friends, and Pete's warning him about buying the class ring because of what his father will say, but then later he sees Clark throw Mr. Kent into the car. Pete starts wondering what the hell is going on — he's trying to be a friend to his friend, but he also wants to be a friend to his friend's father, so he's totally in the middle."

Sam thinks that Pete's decision shines light on a strong part of Pete himself. "I think it was very brave of him to go on the journey with Jonathan Kent," he says, recalling the scene where Pete exposes Clark to the green kryptonite to weaken him sufficiently in order to allow Jonathan to destroy the red ring. "He had to make his friend feel pain in order to get better. Opening the box with the kryptonite was hard for Pete, but he had to do it. Jonathan Kent has unbelievable love for Clark, and I think he knows that Pete has the same amount of love."

Of course, Pete's knowledge of Clark's weaknesses proves dangerous for the Kents in 'Rush', an episode which Sam Jones really enjoyed working on. "Allison and I just had a *blast* on that," he laughs. "From beginning to end, it was nothing but action — it was really fun. The only part that I didn't have much fun with, which I had to fake looking pleased about, was when we jumped the car off of the cliff. In a couple of episodes, Allison has been in those wires where she's hanging off the ground, so she's used to it. But that was my first time, and I was up in a car that weighed a couple of thousand pounds, which was only being held by a couple of wires and a crane — and I was ten feet up in the air. People got a kick out of watching me go up there and be so scared. Allison was telling me to relax, but I told her I was scared. When they called 'action', I was going 'Whooh! This is so fun!' but as soon as they said 'cut!', I was going, 'Get me down out of here — hurry up and get this thing *down!*"

The second season doesn't see Sam getting much chance of a romance. He still has the strong friendship with Chloe that developed through the first season, but unlike in the DC Comics continuity, where Pete and Lana briefly ended up married, the second season sees very few scenes shared by Sam and Kristin Kreuk. "When we got the call sheet showing who's working each day on an episode, usually she was working when I was not," Sam points out. "I think that Pete just sees Lana as the girl that Clark has the hots for. They're friends, but not as good as Pete and Clark are, or Pete and Chloe are. They know each other, and he knows that she's smart, and a nice girl, but I don't think he has any other interest in her."

Pete has many opportunities during the second year to demonstrate what Sam Jones considers to be one of his best qualities — his smile. "He's such a warm, nice friend, and a good person," he explains. "I didn't realize how important smiles were until I started working on this show. When Allison comes to work, she gives some of the biggest smiles I've ever seen! You can be in any mood, but those smiles touch you in a way that she's not even aware of. It's just a habit she has. I tried to do that with Pete on the show — the action and the scenes are great, but I think the big moments are when Clark and Pete share a smile."

Sam is well aware of Pete's role in the drama — "Superman doesn't have a sidekick," he notes — and is very grateful to the fans of the show for the support that they give him. "They really were a major part in Pete's finding out the secret," he says, "and I thank them every time I go to a convention, because they helped that happen for me." ∎

CHLOE SULLIVAN

"I want to let you in on a secret. I'm not who you think I am. In fact, my disguise is so thin, I'm surprised you haven't seen right through me. I'm the girl of your dreams masquerading as your best friend."

"The first season was the brain, the second season was the heart for Chloe," Allison Mack maintains, assessing the difference between the hardheaded investigative reporter that the *Smallville* audience saw in the first year of the show, and the rather lovelorn teenager of the second year.

Allison enjoys playing Chloe best when there is a "strict balance" of her brain and her heart. "Too much of one thing could be really boring," she points out. "It's been great being able to play some of the 'heart', and have Chloe as this angsty teenager."

The actress was "a little disappointed that Chloe lost some of her backbone" in the second year, but very pleased that "she got it back in the end and redeemed herself. She was a little spineless and a little bit too much of a pushover. I wanted her to just suck it up and go forward, so it was a little frustrating."

Allison still feels that Chloe is a driven character, and we learn this year that part of that may derive from her home life. In 'Lineage', Chloe tells Clark that her mother walked out, leaving Chloe believing that she wasn't good enough for someone to love. "That was cool — it came from Al, Miles and myself sitting down and them asking what I wanted to see during the second year," Allison recalls. "I thought that Chloe was like this floating head with no real base, and that we should make her a latchkey kid, which explains why she's out all the time after hours. She never really has anybody that she has to report to. She has all these abandonment issues. She feels like she's never good enough, and she's never quite right. That's why it hurts so much when Clark doesn't love her. It's also why she has no female friends, because it's difficult for her to find solace in women, because she doesn't connect with them at all. It was neat to develop that together and then see it come to life and really work."

In the same meeting, Allison asked if she could work more with John Glover as Lionel Luthor, and was therefore delighted when she saw the scripts for the last episodes of season two. "I wanted that, and I was really excited," she says. "It's so different from anything that I had ever played or done. It was going to put such a different spin on my character, as she was definitely going to grow because of it. When she changes and evolves, it's always more interesting than playing the same thing every week. I liked the fact that she just goes to Lionel out of spite. It's very Chloe — she just reacts, she doesn't wait and think things through!"

Allison relishes any chance she can get to work opposite the veteran performer. "Working with John is always such a treat, because he's such a fantastic actor," she comments, "so it's been really nice having the opportunity to play off him, learn from him, and observe him on set."

CHLOE SULLIVAN

Although everyone else calls her Chloe, Lionel refers to her consistently as 'Miss Sullivan'. "That came from John," Allison reveals. "He always calls me 'Miss Mack'!"

Allison was given an opportunity to display other facets of her acting talents when Chloe came under the influence of the parasite from the Kawatche caves in 'Rush'. "It was like playing a totally different character," Allison recalls. "That was a really big challenge for me, because I've never been cast as the sexy girl, or even the really pretty girl. I'm always the cute, quirky sidekick, or the abused girl. I'm never just your run-of-the-mill girlfriend. I've never been comfortable playing that — acting and performing and not having anything other than my appearance to look at. There's always been another layer of really difficult dialog or emotion layered over it. But 'Rush' was all about me being the one that was desired, and it was a challenge for me to be comfortable doing that! It helped that I'm so comfortable with Tom. Kristin and I both say that we're so glad that we do those scenes with Tom — he's so respectful, and wants to make sure that we're comfortable and okay. Any time we have to do any wacky, weird kissing scene, we're always glad it's him!"

She's also delighted to have the opportunity to take part in the stunt sequences, but Allison admits that she would "never fight back when they want my stunt woman Lorelei to do it, because I figure it would hurt. I don't think there's been anything that I've wanted to do but didn't get to do. The one I enjoyed the most was when I jump off the ledge in 'Rush' and ask Clark if he's going to catch me, so I let go, and fall straight back. I went down onto a big padded mat, with a bunch of people holding on to make sure that I didn't fall off the mat. My stunt double did the actual fall, and then they cut to a shot of Tom holding me. Before every take he goes, 'Don't worry, I got it,' and would chuck me up in the air and then catch me! He made me feel really light — that was nice!"

Allison is happy that the show is constantly moving forward, and although she's glad that Chloe is a very independent girl, she would like to "find some sort of common ground for either Martha and Lana, or Martha and Chloe, because I think it's an important element that we haven't explored yet. The relationships are male-female, or male-male. I think that Chloe moving in with Lana was an attempt to try to subtly bring us together and figure out ways of making us closer, because there aren't that many strong female relationships on the show. But there's not a whole lot in common between them, other than Clark."

Allison doesn't think that Clark ever loved Chloe, and doesn't hold out hope that this is going to be the relationship of her life. "I think he has a really strong affection for her, and a lot of times, he confuses that with love because he cares about her so much," she says. "But I don't think he was ever in love with her. Chloe's not his type! He has a lot of strong feelings for her, and he's crazy about her and doesn't want her to go anywhere, but he doesn't lust for her." ▪

LIONEL LUTHOR

"Altruism is not in your blood, Lex. Believe me. I don't know what you're up to, but you found something valuable in those caves, and whatever it is, I'll find it."

During the first season of *Smallville*, Lionel Luthor became an increasing presence within the series, culminating in the teaser to 'Tempest', which was based solely around the power game between Lionel and Lex as Lionel shut down the LuthorCorp plant. Any doubts that the older Luthor might not survive the accident in the library at the end of that episode were dispelled when John Glover appeared in the title sequence to the second season.

Slowly but surely during the second year, Lionel becomes more and more involved with the lives of the people of Smallville, whether directly, by hiring Martha Kent as his assistant during his time 'resting' at the Luthor mansion after his accident, or indirectly through his investigations into the Kawatche caves. "It's happened gradually," John Glover points out, "and it's been quite exciting to feel that we've made Lionel so important. Men of power like to be treated as important, so it's nice!"

Glover considers that Lionel is one of those people who will do whatever is necessary in order to achieve their goals. "He's got his plans," he says, "but he's intelligent enough, and flexible enough, to go where he needs to go. He's so sharp, and he can read people. He's got an instinct about them."

Lionel is quick to recognize other people's potential to help further those plans — such as when Chloe comes to him at the end of the season, bitter at her treatment by Clark and Lana. "He's got a way to get to people, and to somehow get in past their defenses," Glover notes, then adds ruefully, "it's a shame that everything he does is just for himself. He's interested in power, wealth, and money. Just imagine if he were doing everything he does for the benefit of mankind. Think what a mind like that could be doing if it were being used for good! Look at the way he deals with people. It's like anybody powerful — people always end up doing things for them. Lionel couldn't be where he is if he was any other way."

So far, only one person that Lionel wants has got away from his clutches: Martha Kent. Glover thinks that on a personal level, Lionel and Jonathan Kent are rivals for Martha. "We both want the same woman," the actor says bluntly. "Jonathan will never forgive Lionel for certain things." Like Annette O'Toole, Glover enjoyed the scenes in the first part of the season when Martha was working for Lionel. "It was so fascinating to watch where that went," he remembers. "It was disappointing when that came to an end. It was deepening the characters. Annette is such a great actress that the audience wouldn't have had to worry that she couldn't be redeemed. We loved playing together in that incredible little arc. It was wonderful. There's a scene in 'Nocturne' where Lionel comes back from being with Martha, and Lex finds him playing some Chopin on the piano, that was a love poem to her."

LIONEL LUTHOR

The actor doesn't consider that Lionel was being weakened by Martha's attempts to make him do the right thing. "Lionel's the devil in the show," he smiles, "but the more you can make a villain human, the more interesting he is to watch. You're wondering where he's going to go now, what he's going to do next. It's what makes it exciting! I think that Lionel really likes Martha. There's something that she touches in him — a part of himself that she makes feel a certain way, even though he's got everything."

Martha comes to help Lionel after she finds him getting frustrated with the side effects of his blindness, and his seeming inability to be able to work to his fullest potential. Glover is aware that some members of the audience believe that Lionel never lost his vision, and was faking his blindness throughout, rather than, as he claims, finding that his sight returned shortly before the events of 'Prodigal'. However, as far as Glover is concerned, Lionel *was* blind, which posed some practical problems during shooting.

"It took a while to figure out how to 'do' blind for the camera," he remembers. "It didn't look right to me during the first episode. If you've ever spoken to a blind person, you know that they don't look at you directly. But on film in close-ups, it looked like I was still looking at the person I was talking to. So then I tried looking down. In 'Skinwalker', the episode's director, Marita Grabiak, asked me to look at some buttons on the camera, but unfortunately it looked like I could still see. It wasn't until I actually looked to the *opposite* side of the camera to where the person was that it worked. It was as simple a technical thing as that, but it worked!"

Lionel's interest in Clark ("a very interesting young man") starts to grow during the second season, particularly after the events of 'Red' and 'Insurgence', and Glover enjoys the opportunity to work with Tom Welling. "I only have a couple of scenes here and there with Tom during the second year," he notes, "but they give Lionel such juicy stuff with everyone. I've had some great stuff with Allison, and some incredible scenes with Michael and Annette. They're the main people that they let me play with — although I had a nice scene with Sam Jones in 'Exodus' when he gets me to change my focus while Clark comes in and steals the key. That was fun, because I'd never gotten to play with Sam before."

As far as his relationship with Lex is concerned, Glover still feels that Lionel is trying to temper Lex's steel. "Lionel knows that Lex might not believe him, but he knows so well what Lex is feeling about him, and what it means to be 'Lionel Luthor's son'," Glover explains. "When Lionel was the same age as Lex, he was filled with anger against his father, and wanted, more than anything, to distance himself from his father, and everything he represented, just as Lex is now. But before Lionel realized what his father wanted for him, and what his secret hopes were, his father died, and it was too late for Lionel to tell him that he understood. I think Lionel hopes that Lex won't make the same mistake, and will be willing to learn from Lionel. He still loves Lex, in spite of everything."

Glover enjoys going to work on the set in Vancouver, and is delighted at the open communication between actors and producers. "They listen to us and we listen to them," he notes. "That's why things are really good. We're all learning how to work together. They're using our assets, and it's being written more around the acting. The producers are finding out who we are, so it becomes what it's supposed to be. They came up with such great stuff for me during this season and I'm always looking forward to what they have coming up..." ∎

MARTHA KENT

"Clark, we're not trying to keep you from learning about your past. We just don't want to see you get hurt, either."

"I think the interaction of all the characters is really interesting," says Annette O'Toole. "It's fascinating how Jonathan and Martha worry about how they're going to raise this person to whom no rules apply, and yet how normal they are with all these superpowers going on, like superspeed and heat vision, that they have to deal with. There's all this love there."

The second season of *Smallville* gives Martha an opportunity to show that there is more to her life than just looking after Clark. At the start of the year, when Lionel is struck blind after his accident in 'Tempest', she goes to work for the tycoon, over Jonathan's very deeply felt objections. "At the beginning of season two, I went in to have a meeting with Al and Miles," Annette recalls, "and I brought up the idea of Martha going to work for Lex. I said that she wasn't using her degree. She's got a teenager who she doesn't need to be there for every day. Even though her kid is somebody who needs a little more than most teenagers, she and Jonathan are more involved with Clark than most parents would be with their teenagers. In the first season, we were always asking him what he did today, because his powers were just becoming evident. But now the farm seemed to be doing okay, and it seemed to me that I was doing the books on the farm more than anything else. Either I was doing the bills, or I was making muffins, or making coffee!"

She was delighted when the producers ran with her idea, making a few changes along the way. "They took the germ of that idea, and turned it into working for Lionel," she says. "I loved the intrigue of being a little spy, and now knowing that Lionel knows something about Clark. I wanted it to be a bit like the spy shows — I thought it would be great if I was a spy, and Lionel kept catching me, and I kept being caught in lies. I wish I still had stuff to do with John Glover — when my character started to go in this direction, there was never any hint that Martha was going to be seduced to the 'dark side' in any way, but I would read things by fans online saying that the baby was definitely Lionel's!"

Annette was disappointed that the plotline seemed to come to an end at the start of 'Suspect', but hopes that something similar might be picked up again in future episodes — perhaps other opportunities for Martha to display her keen intelligence. "I'd hoped that the secret that Ryan discovered was that she was going to run for mayor," she says. "It would be very difficult because the Kents are trying not to be public people because of their son's secret, but this woman needs an outlet for her intelligence and her abilities."

Annette was not fond of the idea of Martha becoming pregnant. "I felt maybe they were fooling around with the canon too much," she says. "I never felt there was going to be an interesting, good enough end to the story." Martha's pregnancy, revealed in

'Fever', meant that she became increasingly tied to the farm. "When you make a character in their forties who has never had a child pregnant, she's not going to do anything else," she points out. "She's going to stay on the farm. She's going to have to quit her job. I really was disappointed with that storyline — I believed it could paralyze the character." But Annette isn't certain that Martha ever was pregnant. "This is what makes sense to me," she explains. "I think it was an hysterical pregnancy caused by the ship, because it was giving her what she most wanted. That's why I didn't want her to wear the pad, which they had me start wearing."

Inevitably, Martha lost the baby as a result of the truck crash caused by the shockwave released by Clark's destruction of the spaceship. Martha's reaction to Clark as a result also derived from the actress. "How could she blame Clark? She would never blame him," she says firmly. "He did what in his own mind he felt he had to do. This was about him becoming a man. By blowing up the spaceship, he was trying not to cause his parents worry. One of the last things I said to Miles and Al at the end of the second season was that she can't blame him. She's a mother, and Clark is this gift to her. He's the only child she will love."

One of Annette's favorite aspects of working on the show is seeing each character pursuing their own plotline. "I think the episodes that work best are the ones where everybody has something that they're following," she maintains. "Clark is certainly the hub of our wheel, but I thought it was going to be more of an ensemble piece. When Pete found out the secret, I thought that he should be with the Kents in every scene. He's part of our family now — whether he has a line or not, he should be with us. Martha's take on it all is that she wants Clark to be as normal as he can possibly be in this situation. She wants him to have a best friend he can confide all his secrets to. She wants him to have relationship with a girl. She wants him to experience as much of being human as possible. Martha's always the 'yes — go do it' and Jonathan's always the 'no — wait a minute, we've got to think about this.'"

Like John Schneider, Annette enjoys the character-based moments. "I loved the scene in 'Lineage' where the two kids are looking at one another, and Clark reaches over and touches Lex's face," she recalls. "It's the first thing he wakes up

for. Those moments are the ones that I think this show does so beautifully. Greg Beeman directed that episode, and did a beautiful job of that connection from the past."

Annette knows that although John Schneider is very generous in offering to share lines in a scene that the Kent parents have with their son, "most of the time it doesn't make sense for Martha to have certain lines, because they just don't come out of her mouth in the same way. It can put a different spin on the scene that I don't think the writers intended it to have. Our main job is to serve the show and serve the piece and what the writers are saying with it, and a lot of times what they're saying doesn't involve Martha. But why she's *not* speaking is as interesting as what she says sometimes. The other interesting thing of being on the sidelines like that is you can really see what's going on — and that's what's happened with Martha. Sometimes in scenes she's the audience's eyes into what's *really* going on." ∎

JONATHAN KENT

"I let my anger get the best of me. I haven't exactly kept it a secret how Jonathan Kent feels about the Luthors. What jury could possibly believe me now?"

"The challenge for me," John Schneider explains, "is to keep true to who Jonathan is, and to who I've perceived Jonathan to have developed into, within the confines of the story." *Smallville's* second season sees Clark's powers continue to develop, and Jonathan and Martha Kent have to deal with their son's increasing maturity, as well as keeping their home life going. That leads Martha to start working for Lionel Luthor, which in its turn sees Jonathan as the prime suspect after the attempt on the tycoon's life.

Clark also makes some major mistakes during the year, not least during 'Red', and when he destroys the spaceship with the kryptonite key at the end of 'Exodus'. Jonathan is aware that his son has faults, and Schneider enjoys playing the scenes where Jonathan has to deal with letting Clark make his mistakes, even if there are serious consequences. "Nobody wants to send their child out into the world any sooner than they have to," he says, "and even then, they don't really want to send them. We're dealing with letting go from a parent's side, and then asking themselves if they've done the best job they can. The scenes in 'Red' dealt with that so well."

Schneider is pleased that the relationship between Clark and his parents remains on an even keel during the second season. "I get a lot of wonderful comments about the parenting of Martha and Jonathan on this show, from both teenagers and parents," he points out. "The normalcy of the Kent farm is very important. As fantastic as the show can get, there's a very real, solid foundation here — it's like *Little House on the X-Files!* The relationships between Clark and his parents have been defined so well. The audience knows that Clark has a place to go. There are more people who live at the end of a dirt road in our country — in any country — than live somewhere like Metropolis. People identify with the problems the Kent farm has. We maintain a high level of realism, despite being about the adolescence of Superman."

The actor continues his fight to ensure that Clark's problems aren't always the highest item on the agenda for Jonathan and Martha. "It used to drive me crazy when I worked on *Dr. Quinn, Medicine Woman*," he recalls. "I did that show for a year-and-a-half, and my mother said to me once, 'You know, it's pretty amazing that she can deal with typhoid and the Indian problem, and the soldiers raiding town, and still have a twenty-pound turkey on the table by six o'clock!' And I thought, 'You know, mom, you're absolutely right, that completely belies the suspension of disbelief. We as the audience should believe this is really happening, and we're just flies on the wall.' So Annette and I are both very aware of trying to keep a realistic life [for our characters] outside of what's happening with Clark."

The episodes that are closer to Schneider's heart are the ones that are more character-based than plot-driven, particularly any which demonstrate the lengths to which Jonathan will go to in order to keep Clark safe. "Creatively, the writers and producers come up with stories, and fit the characters into them," he notes, "and occasionally they might come up with a story around the characters, but that's not the norm. I loved 'Vortex', because any time that you see a parent willing to go to jail, or experience some discomfort because they love their child, is great. That's what real life is. It is abundantly clear in that episode that Jonathan would rather die than let Nixon get out of the crypt and destroy his son's life. That's wonderful, and people need to hear that. They need to know that that's a real parental feeling, and that's not been explored on television. It's like that marvelous movie *John Q*, where it might be a bit wild that the father takes over the hospital to help his son, but what that father did because he loved his son was fantastic."

Jonathan's selflessness is demonstrated in 'Suspect', and one scene in particular sums up the character in the actor's eyes. "I was in a big orange jumpsuit in jail," he says, "and I said to Martha, 'All it takes is one reckless moment to ruin everything.' At those times, it's really obvious that the least important person in Jonathan's life is Jonathan."

Schneider also enjoyed the offbeat episode, 'Visitor'. "I was only in it for about a heartbeat," he recalls, "with the young man who thought he was an alien too, and had the healing powers. I think the thread that ties my favorite shows together is that they are more about heart than they are about solving the problem. It's nice to have about four 'Freak of the Week' shows in a season and go to that weird place, but other than that, I think that's enough."

Although he didn't travel to New York for the filming of 'Rosetta', Schneider is delighted that Christopher Reeve made a guest appearance on the series. "I looked on that as being a seal of approval," he notes. "With what that man has been through, and what he was continually going through, it's amazing. On the professional side, what an incredible coup it was to have Chris be on *Smallville*."

Schneider admits that "occasionally the show will take Jonathan and Martha's relationship with Clark somewhere it wouldn't really go, and we have to be the 'police'

of the perceived morality of this family, or it'll become like every other television show, where if it wasn't for the innate intelligence of the teenager, the parents couldn't make it through the day!" However the actor is "proud of everything that I've done on this show. I'm proud of every relationship. We've had a taste of such great relationships that I can't wait for more things to happen. I'd like to see Lana and Chloe have interaction with Jonathan and Martha. Lana's whole lament has been that she doesn't have a family, and I would think that she would like to talk to Jonathan about how a father could walk away from his daughter. I would have liked to have had a conversation with Pete where he found out that it was our fault that his dad sold the creamed corn factory to Lionel Luthor."

He thinks the continuing success of the show is because "no matter what happens in people's lives, I think that somewhere inside all of us, even the bad people believe that when push comes to shove, good will win out over evil. This show explores that, and we explore how someone can be devoted to doing the right thing, even at his own expense. Exploring this whole theme through the eyes of a teenager is really striking a chord in teenagers *and* parents. I'm delighted to be a part of that." ■

MEET THE CREW

"When people say *Smallville* is about family, they don't realize that that 'family' goes right down to the very roots of the show... the crew — this incredibly supportive, caring, creative and funny group of people who take care of us all." — John Glover

It takes hundreds of people to bring an episode of *Smallville* to life: not only the actors, crew, technical and support personnel at *Smallville*'s studios in Burnaby, British Columbia, but also the writers, producers, and support staff based at the series' Los Angeles offices. While many members of the team have already been introduced in the course of the episode entries earlier in the book, this section is a chance to focus in more detail on the roles of some key personnel. Everyone has an essential part to play...

David Willson has been *Smallville*'s production designer since the start of the second season. "I get a story outline usually a month or so in front of the script," he explains. "I'll then start mobilizing location folks to find locations that fit that outline. If they look like they're too difficult to find, we'll redirect the writers to create something that we can actually do. Maybe there's a pressure on that kind of location in town, or it's way beyond our budget means — at that point, we get the writers to redirect the script a bit."

As Vancouver has a busy film industry, some of the high-tech locations are in great demand. "Often a reoccurring location has been booked by another production," Willson says. "We've had several locations that we've established as LuthorCorp or Lex's mansion that we tried to go back to, but other productions have booked subsequent to our shoot. Metropolis particularly is a tough one to find."

By the time Willson receives a script, "I've seen some of the locations, and we've started some preliminary ideas about sets that we can't find, so we have to build on our stages. We rough out some floor plans to fit those ideas. Then we start scouting with the director, usually eight days before we start shooting, locking down our locations, working out how to alter them if necessary, and figuring the sets that need to be built. Most of our directors are reoccurring, so they're pretty much familiar with our 'menu'."

It's Willson's responsibility to oversee the visual aspects of the filming, and maintain a continuity from episode to episode. "The costumes and locations need to fit into our visual pallet," he explains. "It's a much happier pallet than other shows that have filmed in Vancouver, like *The X-Files*, *Millennium*, and *Dark Angel*. Depending on the mood of the script, whether it's dark, light, or romantic, each aspect of our story has a different pallet. We see Smallville itself in a series of circles, with the Kent farm being the center of the universe in terms of the Kents. It's very warm, encompassing and family-oriented, and you get a lot of light. The further you get from that circle and get into Smallville itself, it starts to mix the colors a bit, and as you get further from that into Metropolis, and the Luthor world, it gets darker. It's edgier, a little scarier, and not quite as inviting."

Christopher Sayour is one of the stunt coordinators on the series, alongside Tony

Above: On location, setting up a shot.

Morelli, and also acts as Tom Welling's stunt double for those scenes that are too dangerous for Tom to try. With the arrival of films like *The Matrix*, where so many stunts can only be achieved with the assistance of computer generated effects, Sayour enjoys working with producer Bob Hargrove, because Hargrove loves to see a stunt done live, on the set. "He likes to do it practically," Sayour confirms. "He'll add CG where it has to be, or where we couldn't shoot something because of time problems, but I like the fact that he looks at me and Tony and says, 'Let's do the full-on deal!' Everybody's testing the boundaries with CG, and it is our friend to a point, especially with digital wire removal, since we can use thicker cable, so we can do bigger gags. But if you enhance a gag with CG too far, it just looks stupid."

Like many stunt artists, Sayour is keen not to destroy the mystery about when something is done by the actor and when it's done by a stuntman, and the cast on *Smallville* are all game to try to do the stunts themselves when they can. "The only reason the actors are in a position where they can do a stunt, like Allison did in season one's 'Hothead' [wearing a flaming jacket], is because we are right next to them — in that particular case, right next to them holding a fire extinguisher!" Sayour points out. "We guide them through it, and talk them through everything. We've trained them how to do this stuff. They do it because they have faith that we will take care of them and make sure they're okay."

Some of the most daring stunts are described in the episode entries, but Sayour adds this note of caution: "The stunts come off safely and easily because we've trained for years to make this happen. Anybody that would try this stuff normally is bound to get hurt. Even the best, most trained, professional stunt people can, and do, get hurt. The average person who has no training, and hasn't learned all of the knowledge and hasn't trained their body to the point of taking the forces involved is going to get injured. This should never be something that you do without an immense amount of training — and that means, basically, learning off all the other stunt people."

Mike Walls came on board *Smallville* as supervisor of special effects starting with 'Leech'. "This is the one show where I can honestly say that we make mini-movies," he says. "I've talked with countless friends of mine who are within the industry who aren't on the show, but have seen or heard what we're doing, and they shake their heads. We're pulling off big stuff. I can count just two episodes that have been light for us. Other than that, a normal episode for us is two or three major gags, and probably four or five smaller things that usually end up causing more problems than they're worth!"

Walls is responsible for the physical effects that happen on the show — such as the pyrotechnics that often characterize the final battle between Clark and the 'Freak of the Week', or demonstrations of Clark's superstrength. In 'Vortex', for example, he had to work out a way for Clark to flip the motor home off the crypt where Jonathan and Nixon are trapped. "Greg Beeman asked how I was going to do it," he recalls, "and I said, 'The thing weighs 15,000 pounds, so I'm going to pick it up on two wires on a crane and I'm going to try and flip it over.' I talked to the crane operator at length about it, and he said, 'Well, if we do it this way at this kind of speed, we should be able to get something to happen.' So I told Christopher Sayour, 'Just go with it and make sure your hands don't leave it until you feel that it's going past center, and then push it away.' And on-screen, it looks like he picks it up! When that thing collapsed down, I couldn't believe how perfect it looked in terms of the way it flattened out. It was better than anything I had ever imagined!"

A physical effect on the set will be enhanced by the visual effects team, or if something goes wrong and there are severe time pressures, they can even create it from scratch. "There's so much interaction between the CG people and us, there's hardly any episode that both aren't involved in to some degree," Walls notes.

John Wash, visual effects supervisor since the Santa Monica-based company Entity FX took over responsibility for the visual effects at the start of the second season, would agree. "My function is to be present on set when scenes that involve visual effects are photographed," he explains. "One of the things that's terrific about *Smallville* is that not only does Clark have the powers they've introduced on the series, but they're always introducing new powers. Every episode involves some kind of visual effect, either with Clark or the people he comes up against. I make sure the material is photographed in the correct way, so we can get the maximum value and effect out of what we are going to digitally add to the shot later, down in Santa Monica."

Opposite: Flipping the motorhome over. Easy when you know how!

Just because a power is used once doesn't mean it'll be the same next time it appears. "We used the material from the first season as a template," Wash notes, "and made some improvements on things that had been established, like X-ray vision. We were able to introduce heat vision, but since then we've gone on from the 'mark one' heat vision, and developed it. We're constantly trying to push the envelope and improve things that we've already established, and tweak them to make them a little bit more exciting. Clark has this tool kit of powers, but we want to make them as varied as we can, so they are new and fresh for the audience."

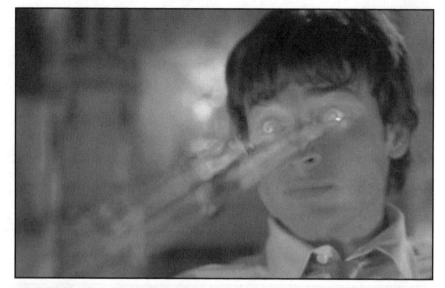

Right: Heat vision in operation at the Talon.

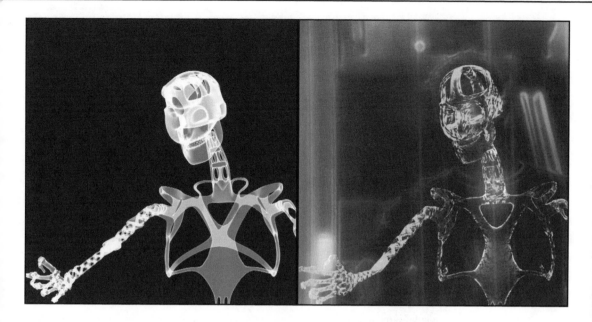

Visual effects producer and supervisor **Mat Beck** visits the set if there's a very complicated sequence being shot, but is more normally found at Entity FX's offices on a suburban road in Santa Monica. Entity had previously been responsible for the effects on *The X-Files*, but found their work very different on *Smallville*. "*The X-Files* happens a lot in the dark, and there's a lot of detail hidden in the shadows," he explains. "In *Smallville*, whatever weird stuff is happening, the town looks great. It's bright and sunny, so with a few exceptions, most things tend to happen in full view, and you see a lot of detail. But what *The X-Files* and *Smallville* have in common is that they're both made by groups of really smart people, who are creative and collaborative. We like the flow of creative energy that goes in both directions."

Beck works closely with executive producers Alfred Gough and Miles Millar, and with Greg Beeman and the production crew when they are developing a new effect, but usually coordinates with Ken Horton during post-production. Because there is a limited amount of time for them to work on effects (and it's not unusual for a shot for next Wednesday's episode to still be on the computers on the Friday beforehand), "we often have parallel approaches and see which works. Sometimes our two-dimensional department and our three-dimensional department will be trying something at the same time. Sometimes we'll have two different 3D approaches.

"When someone is watching the episode on a Wednesday night, or five years from then," Beck concludes, "they're not going to be interested in the story of how the show was 'pretty good considering how little time there was', and the difficulties. Nobody wants to know about that — you put the image up there and it speaks for itself." ∎

Above: Two stages in creating the X-ray vision effect.

THE CHLOE CHRONICLES

"On October 16, 1989, Smallville became Meteor Capital of the World. Ever since that day our little town has been besieged by a staggering number of seemingly inexplicable and allegedly unrelated events. I should know. I've been keeping score..."

During the closing part of the second season, fans of the series were able to get an extra fix of *Smallville* on top of the regular episodes, as AOL, and later the Channel 4 website in Britain, hosted a series of promotional webisodes centering around the character of Chloe Sullivan. After an introductory speech to the camera, Chloe and her unnamed cameraman started to investigate the case of Earl Jenkins, the janitor from the LuthorCorp plant who was affected with the jitters in the first season episode, and discovered links to Dr. Steven Hamilton and a mysterious cloning project involving the green meteor rocks...

"Mark Warshaw, who is in charge of the websites and the DVDs, had an idea to do an interactive website with myself and the show," Allison Mack recalls. "It would explain the unexplained, and finish some unfinished business online, utilizing my character and a digital camera. *The Chloe Chronicles* gives people a chance to check out more in-depth details on *Smallville* and Chloe. She is digging a little deeper into all the mysterious

Right: Chloe explains her mission.

Above: The enigmatic Dr. Jamison and widow Belinda Jenkins.

things that happen around Smallville. On the TV show, people die nearly every week, but nobody goes to interview the family, or tries to figure out what's happened, so that's what Chloe decides she's going to do — except instead of writing it, she puts it on video."

Allison enjoyed shooting the promos in and around *Smallville*'s studio. "It's fun — it gives us a lot more focus on Chloe," she says. "It's very Nancy Drew and mysterious. I think it's a bit more like *The X-Files* or *NYPD Blue*. The *Chronicles* are like a detective story, with Chloe following clues and interviewing people, going from spot to spot, figuring things out."

The first volume of *Chronicles* foreshadowed some of the developments within the series in the third year, as Chloe tries to uncover exactly what LuthorCorp is up to. "It's really neat," Allison says, "because Mark works so closely with Al and Miles, so they're always communicating and getting ideas back and forth from each other."

The scripts for these web promos were written by Brice Tidwell, with Lucia Walters returning to reprise her role as Belinda Jenkins from 'Jitters', and Christopher Heyerdahl and Gerard Plunket playing Chloe's targets of investigation.

"I have script approval, so I get to look at them, and make changes before anything happens," Allison notes. "I definitely have a hand in the way that it sounds and the way that it goes. Mark is very much a team player, and wants everyone to be as excited and passionate about it as he is. I've had a lot more input into *The Chloe Chronicles* than into *Smallville* simply because it's more about me! We have time to get me involved."

Mark Warshaw wants to continue tying all the different outside elements of the series together. "I go to Al and Miles and the writers and continually try to figure out how to expand their stories in an online sense," he says. "They're so open to giving something extra to the fans." ■

THE PHENOMENON

"It's reached the pinnacle of pop culture success... *Smallville* is maturing nicely" — *Entertainment Weekly*

Season two of *Smallville* was even more successful than the first in more ways than one. Ratings-wise, the figures were there in black and white: "*Smallville*... is quickly emerging as the [WB's] biggest hit ever, surpassing even the wholesome stalwart *7th Heaven*," industry bible *The Hollywood Reporter* noted approvingly. "This week's episode — in which young Kent's life goes haywire after he dons a ring laced with kryptonite — propelled The WB to its highest ever rating in the key adults 18-34 demo, with a 5.4 rating/15 share. That was an increase of 46% over last season's average for *Smallville's* original episodes, according to figures from Nielsen Media Reseach."

Creatively too, the show was going from strength to strength, refining its approach to the characters and striking a chord with more and more viewers in the process. "It was a little bit of a rollback to do that perfect mom and dad stuff," says Joe Davola, Head of Television Production at Tollin Robbins, looking back over the second year, "but people seem to love it, seem to crave it. It seems like they're looking for that normality in their lives. Even with a son that's a freak, the parents will do whatever needs to be done for him. I think people are yearning to see that in their lives."

"*Smallville's* biggest achievement... may be its creative rebirth," Bruce Fretts wrote in *Entertainment Weekly*. "Once overreliant on F/X, the plots have dug deeper into its core characters' back stories this season, yielding richer episodes. Now the mutant-centric stories, like the recent episode in which *Home Improvement* vet Jonathan Taylor Thomas played a brainiac who cloned himself so he could two-time Lana and classmate Chloe Sullivan, are used more sparingly. And that leaves more screen time for the regular characters to get their freak on."

For those desperate for new adventures of their heroes, the gap between seasons one and two was partly filled with the release of the first novels based on the series. Two ranges were created — a young adult series, which began with a novelization of the pilot, including some further deleted scenes, and an adult series, which attracted authors including the well-known comic book writers Roger Stern, Alan Grant, and Devin Grayson. Eighteen books have been published across the two ranges. And, of course, the history of the show is now being chronicled in the official companion series, as well as the official magazine.

Clark Kent has also returned to his comic book roots with the publication of a *Smallville* comic, which began with a special issue, and then started bimonthly issues in May 2003. The stories are penned by writers on the show, including 'Rogue' author Mark Verheiden (who has contributed a story set within that episode), season one scripter Michael Green, and 'Precipice' writer Clint Carpenter, who has taken the reins

Opposite: One example of the merchandise now available to the Smallville *fan: action figures.*

for the majority of the issues. As the comic book has progressed, the creators have taken the opportunity to tie it closely into the series continuity, showing what Chloe got up to at the *Daily Planet* between 'Vortex' and 'Heat', and some of Clark's adventures in Metropolis following the events of 'Exodus'.

During the year the officially created online *Smallville Ledger* and *Torch* (from which excerpts appear alongside most episode entries in this book) continued to provide further background information on the world of Smallville, while fan sites such as KryptonSite had to increase their bandwidth to accommodate the sheer volume of interest in the series.

Numerous tie-in items also began to appear. Fans could eat their lunch from their *Smallville* lunchbox, and swap their trading cards while gazing at their posters of assorted members of the cast, and listening to the *Talon Mix*, a CD selection of the most popular tracks from the show, including Remy Zero's opening song, and Five For Fighting's 'Superman' (which at one stage was considered as a possible theme). They could even create adventures of their own with action figures of the cast, including a fully poseable Clark Kent! "He looks a bit awkward," Tom Welling told *Entertainment Weekly* soon after its release. "I grew up with G. I. Joe and He-Man, and they were big and strong. But Clark is awkward on the show."

Although there was nearly a year between the end of the season and the release of the DVD box set in May 2004, it was worth the wait for fans. As well as widescreen transfers of the episodes, they got a chance to see a number of deleted scenes, as well as hear commentaries from members of the cast and crew on two of the key episodes of the year, 'Heat' and 'Rosetta'. And as the start of the third season approached, telephone company Verizon was involved with a series of short vignettes that hinted strongly at the troubled times ahead for Clark in Metropolis... ▪

23 More Things I Learned This School Year

By Chloe Sullivan

Lesson 1: When sucked into a vortex, better hope you have a friend to pull you out.

Lesson 2: If you can't stand the heat, stay away from the Kent barn, Ms. Atkins' Sex Ed class, and the SHS electronics shop classroom.

Lesson 3: Duplicity between friends will ruin the friendship.

Lesson 4: Red is a pretty color for a stone, as long as it's a real ruby.

Lesson 5: Whether painted, written or composed, a nocturne will first seem dark and frightening, but often holds great beauty when you give it a chance.

Lesson 6: If something has to be redux, there's a good chance it sucks (but sometimes not as badly as you first thought).

Lesson 7: You cannot choose your lineage, you can only do the best with the one that you have.

Lesson 8: Ryan James taught us all a lot about the fragility of life and the wonder of the mind.

Lesson 9: That which is dichotic plays pending to perspective.

Lesson 10: The Kawatche people once roamed Smallville and were Skinwalkers — meaning Smallville was ground zero for the bizarre, long before the meteors landed here.

Lesson 11: The visage is not always what it first seems.

Lesson 12: Insurgence is dangerous, but at times necessary to uncover the Truth.

Lesson 13: Suspect authority.

Lesson 14: Rush is achieved when inhibition is squashed.

Lesson 15: When the prodigal son returns, send him back.

Lesson 16: If you have a fever, get rest, drink lots of fluids and hope for a really bright light.

Lesson 17: The Rosetta Stone was a basalt tablet bearing inscriptions in Greek, Egyptian hieroglyphics and demotic scripts that was discovered in 1799 near Rosetta, a town of northern Egypt in the Nile River delta, and provided the key to the decipherment of Egyptian hieroglyphics. (Websters)

Lesson 18: We have many strange things in Smallville, but a visitor from outer space living among us is not one of them.

Lesson 19: When reaching a precipice, sometimes you need to take the law into your own hands.

Lesson 20: When you witness a crime, you need to report it. (Especially to our new sheriff.)

Lesson 21: To accelerate growth beyond that which nature intended will open up Pandora's box.

Lesson 22: Either heed your calling or shut it up!

Lesson 23: When mass exodus occurs from all that you know, all that you trust, all that you believe in... fear not, for there is a plan, there is a roadmap, and disappointment is not part of it...

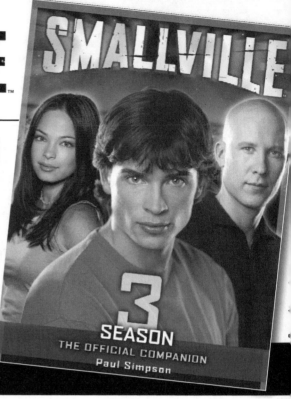